Allyn and Bacon

Quick Guide to the Internet
for
Social Work

2000 Edition

Joanne Yaffe

University of Utah

Doug Gotthoffer

California State University–Northridge

Allyn and Bacon

Boston • London • Toronto • Sydney • Tokyo • Singapore

Senior Series Editor: Judy Fifer
Multimedia Developmental Editor: Nina Tisch
Editorial Production: Marla Feuerstein
Cover Designer: Jennifer Hart
Editorial Production Service: Omegatype Typography, Inc.

NOTICE: Between the time Web site information is gathered and then published, it is not unusual for some sites to have ceased operating. Also, the transcription of URLs can result in unintended typographical errors. The Publisher would appreciate notification where these occcur so that they may be corrected in subsequent editions. Thank you.

In its effort to provide a diverse list of Web sites, the Publisher has included links that do not necessarily represent the views of Allyn and Bacon. Faculty, students, and researchers are strongly advised to use their analytical skills to determine the truth, accuracy, and value of the content in individual Web sites.

TRADEMARK CREDITS: Where information was available, trademarks and registered trademarks are indicated below. When detailed information was not available, the publisher has indicated trademark status with an initial capital where those names appear in the text.

Macintosh is a registered trademark of Apple Computer, Inc.

Microsoft is a registered trademark of Microsoft Corporation. Windows, Windows95, and Microsoft Internet Explorer are trademarks of Microsoft Corporation.

Netscape and the Netscape Navigator logo are registered trademarks of Netscape Communications Corporation.

Copyright © 2000 by Allyn and Bacon
A Pearson Education Company
Needham Heights, Massachusetts 02494
Internet: www.abacon.com

ISBN 0-205-30967-4

Printed in the United States of America

10 9 8 7 6 5 4 3 2   02 01 00 99

Contents

Introduction to the Internet

You're about to embark on an exciting experience as you become one of the millions of citizens of the Internet. In spite of what you might have heard, the Internet can be mastered by ordinary people before they earn a college degree and even if they're not majoring in rocket science.

Some Things You Ought to Know

Much of the confusion over the Internet comes from two sources. One is terminology. Just as the career you're preparing for has its own special vocabulary, so does the Internet. You'd be hard pressed to join in the shoptalk of archeologists, librarians, or carpenters if you didn't speak their language. Don't expect to plop yourself down in the middle of the Internet without some buzzwords under your belt, either.

The second source of confusion is that there are often many ways to accomplish the same ends on the Internet. This is a direct by-product of the freedom so highly cherished by Net citizens. When someone has an idea for doing something, he or she puts it out there and lets the Internet community decide its merits. As a result, it's difficult to put down in writing the *one exact* way to send email or find information on slugs or whatever.

In addition, there are differences in the workings of a PC or Mac and the various versions of the two major browsers, Netscape Communicator (or Navigator) and Internet Explorer. If you can't find a particular command or function mentioned in the book on your computer, chances are it's there, but in a different place or with a slightly different name. Check the manual or online help that came with your computer, or ask a more computer-savvy friend or professor.

And relax. Getting up to speed on the Internet takes a little time, but the effort will be well rewarded. Approach learning your way around the Internet with the same enthusiasm and curiosity you approach learning your way around a new college campus. This isn't a competition. Nobody's keeping score. And the only winner will be you.

In *Understanding Media,* Marshall McLuhan presaged the existence of the Internet when he described electronic media as an extension of our central nervous system. On the other hand, today's students introduced to the Internet for the first time describe it as "Way cool."

No matter which description you favor, you are immersed in a period in our culture that is transforming the way we live by transforming the nature of the information we live by. As recently as 1980, intelligence was marked by "knowing things." If you were born in that year, by the time you were old enough to cross the street by yourself, that definition had changed radically. Today, in a revolution that makes McLuhan's vision tangible, events, facts, rumors, and gossip are distributed instantly to all parts of the global body. The effects are equivalent to a shot of electronic adrenaline. No longer the domain of the privileged few, information is shared by all the inhabitants of McLuhan's global village. Meanwhile, the concept of information as intelligence feels as archaic as a television remote control with a wire on it (ask your parents about that).

With hardly more effort than it takes to rub your eyes open in the morning you can connect with the latest news, with gossip about your favorite music group or TV star, with the best places to eat on spring break, with the weather back home, or with the trials and tribulations of that soap opera character whose life conflicts with your history class.

You can not only carry on a real-time conversation with your best friend at a college half a continent away, but you can see and hear her, too. Or, you can play interactive games with a dozen or more worldwide, world-class, challengers; and that's just for fun.

When it comes to your education, the Internet has shifted the focus from amassing information to putting that information to use. Newspaper and magazine archives are now almost instantly available, as are the contents of many reference books. Distant and seemingly unapproachable experts are found answering questions in discussion groups or in electronic newsletters.

The Internet also addresses the major problem facing all of us in our split-second, efficiency-rated culture: Where do we find the time? The

part

1

Internet allows professors and students to keep in touch, to collaborate and learn, without placing unreasonable demands on individual schedules. Professors are posting everything from course syllabi to homework solutions on the Internet, and are increasingly answering questions on-line, all in an effort to ease the pressure for face-to-face meetings by supplementing them with cyberspace offices. The Internet enables students and professors to expand office hours into a twenty-four-hour-a-day, seven-day-a-week operation. Many classes have individual sites at which enrolled students can gather electronically to swap theories, ideas, resources, gripes, and triumphs.

By freeing us from some of the more mundane operations of information gathering, and by sharpening our information-gathering skills in other areas, the Internet encourages us to be more creative and imaginative. Instead of devoting most of our time to gathering information and precious little to analyzing and synthesizing it, the Internet tips the balance in favor of the skills that separate us from silicon chips. Other Internet citizens can gain the same advantage, however, and as much as the Internet ties us together, it simultaneously emphasizes our individual skills—our ability to connect information in new, meaningful, and exciting ways. Rarely have we had the opportunity to make connections and observations on such a wide range of topics, to create more individual belief systems, and to chart a path through learning that makes information personally useful and meaningful.

A Brief History of the Internet

The 20th century's greatest advance in personal communication and freedom of expression began as a tool for national defense. In the mid-1960s, the Department of Defense was searching for an information analogy to the new Interstate Highway System, a way to move computations and computing resources around the country in the event the Cold War caught fire. The immediate predicament, however, had to do with the Defense Department's budget, and the millions of dollars spent on computer research at universities and think tanks. Much of these millions was spent on acquiring, building, or modifying large computer systems to meet the demands of the emerging fields of computer graphics, artificial intelligence, and multiprocessing (where one computer was shared among dozens of different tasks).

While this research was distributed across the country, the unwieldy, often temperamental, computers were not. Though researchers at MIT had spare time on their computer, short of packing up their notes and traveling to Massachusetts, researchers at Berkeley had no way to use it. Instead, Berkeley computer scientists would wind up duplicating MIT hardware in California. Wary of being accused of re-inventing the wheel, the Advanced Research Projects Agency (ARPA), the funding arm of the Defense Department, invested in the ARPANET, a private network that would allow disparate computer systems to communicate with each other. Researchers could remain ensconced among their colleagues at their home campuses while using computing resources at government research sites thousands of miles away.

A small cadre of ARPANET citizens soon began writing computer programs to perform little tasks across the Internet. Most of these programs, while ostensibly meeting immediate research needs, were written for the challenge of writing them. These programmers, for example, created the first email systems. They also created games like Space Wars and Adventure. Driven in large part by the novelty and practicality of email, businesses and institutions accepting government research funds begged and borrowed their way onto the ARPANET, and the number of connections swelled.

part

1

As the innocence of the 1960s gave way the business sense of the 1980s, the government eased out of the networking business, turning the ARPANET (now Internet) over to its users. While we capitalize the word "Internet", it may surprise you to learn there is no "Internet, Inc.," no business in charge of this uniquely postmodern creation. Administration of this world-wide communication complex is still handled by the cooperating institutions and regional networks that comprise the Internet. The word "Internet" denotes a specific interconnected network of networks, and not a corporate entity.

Using the World Wide Web for Research

Just as no one owns the worldwide communication complex that is the Internet, there is no formal organization among the collection of hundreds of thousands of computers that make up the part of the Net called the World Wide Web.

If you've never seriously used the Web, you are about to take your first steps on what can only be described as an incredible journey. Initially, though, you might find it convenient to think of the Web as a giant television network with millions of channels. It's safe to say that, among all these channels, there's something for you to watch. Only, how to find it? You could click through the channels one by one, of course, but by the time you found something of interest it would (1) be over or (2) leave you wondering if there wasn't something better on that you're missing.

A more efficient way to search for what you want would be to consult some sort of TV listing. While you could skim through pages more rapidly than channels, the task would still be daunting. A more creative approach would allow you to press a button on your remote control that would connect you to a channel of interest; what's more, that channel would contain the names (or numbers) of other channels with similar programs. Those channels in turn would contain information about other channels. Now you could zip through this million-channel universe, touching down only at programs of potential interest. This seems far more effective than the hunt-and-peck method of the traditional couch potato.

If you have a feel for how this might work for television, you have a feel for what it's like to journey around (or surf) the Web. Instead of channels on the Web, we have *Web sites*. Each site contains one or more *pages*. Each page may contain, among other things, links to other pages, either in the same site or in other sites, anywhere in the world. These other pages may elaborate on the information you're looking at or may direct you to related but not identical information, or even provide contrasting or contradictory points of view; and, of course, these pages could have links of their own.

Web sites are maintained by businesses, institutions, affinity groups, professional organizations, government departments, and ordinary people anxious to express opinions, share information, sell products, or provide services. Because these Web sites are stored electronically, updating them is more convenient and practical than updating printed media. That makes Web sites far more dynamic than other types of research material you may be used to, and it means a visit to a Web site can open up new opportunities that weren't available as recently as a few hours ago.

Hypertext and Links

The invention that unveils these revolutionary possibilities is called *hypertext*. Hypertext is a technology for combining text, graphics, sounds, video, and links on a single World Wide Web page. Click on a link and you're transported, like Alice falling down the rabbit hole, to a new page, a new address, a new environment for research and communication.

Links come in three flavors: text, picture, and hot spot. A text link may be a letter, a word, a phrase, a sentence, or any contiguous combination of text characters. You can identify text links at a glance because

Text
Link

Picture
Link

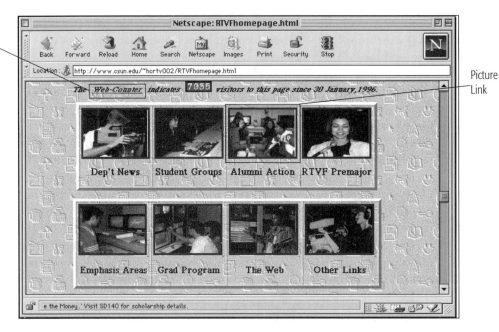

Text links are underlined and set of in color. Picture links are set off by a colored border. Hot spots carry no visual identification.

the characters are <u>underlined</u>, and are often displayed in a unique color, setting the link apart from the rest of the text on the page. Picture links are pictures or other graphic elements. On the Web, a picture may not only be worth a thousand words, but it may also be the start of a journey into a whole new corner of cyberspace.

The third kind of link, the hot spot, is neither underlined nor bordered, a combination which would make it impossible to spot, were it not for a Web convention that offers you a helping hand finding all types of links. This helping hand is, well, a hand. Whenever the mouse cursor passes over a link, the cursor changes from an arrow to a hand. Wherever you see the hand icon, you can click and retrieve another Web page. Sweep the cursor over an area of interest, see the hand, follow the link, and you're surfing the Web.

In the Name of the Page

Zipping around the Web in this way may seem exciting, even serendipitous, but it's also fraught with perils. How, for instance, do you revisit a page of particular interest? Or share a page with a classmate? Or cite a page as a reference for a professor? Web page designers assign names, or titles, to their pages; unfortunately, there's nothing to prevent two designers from assigning the same title to different pages.

An instrument that uniquely identifies Web pages does exist. It's called a Universal Resource Locator (URL), the cyber-signposts of the World Wide Web. URLs contain all the information necessary to locate:

- the page containing the information you're looking for;
- the computer that hosts (stores) that page of information;
- the form the information is stored in.

A typical URL looks like this:

```
http://www.abacon.com/index.html
```

You enter it into the **Location** or **Address** field at the top of your browser window. Hit the **Return** (or **Enter**) key and your browser will deliver to your screen the exact page specified. When you click on a link, you're actually using a shorthand alternative to typing the URL yourself because the browser does it for you. In fact, if you watch the "Location" or "Address" field when you click on a link, you'll see its contents change to the URL you're traveling to.

part

1

The URL Exposed

How does your browser—or the whole World Wide Web structure, for that matter—know where you're going? As arcane as the URL appears, there is a logical explanation to its apparent madness. (This is true not only of URLs but also of your computer experience in general. Because a computer's "intelligence" only extends to following simple instructions exactly, most of the commands, instructions, and procedures you'll encounter have simple underlying patterns. Once you familiarize yourself with these patterns, you'll find you're able to make major leaps in your understanding of new Internet features.)

To unscramble the mysteries of World Wide Web addresses, we'll start at the end of the URL and work our way toward the front.

```
/index.html
```

This is the name of a single file or document. Eventually, the contents of this file/document will be transferred over the Internet to your computer.

However, because there are undoubtedly thousands of files on the Internet with this name, we need to clarify our intentions a bit more.

```
www.abacon.com
```

This is the name of a particular Internet *Web server,* a computer whose job it is to forward Web pages to you on request. By Internet convention, this name is unique. The combination of

```
www.abacon.com/index.html
```

identifies a unique file/document on a unique Web server on the World Wide Web. No other file has this combined address, so there's no question about which file/document to transfer to you.

The characters *http://* at the beginning of the URL identify the method by which the file/document will be transferred. The letters stand for HyperText Transfer Protocol.

Quick Check

Don't Be Lost In (Hyper)Space

Let's pause for a quick check of your Web navigation skills. Look at the sample web page on the next page. How many links does it contain?

Did you find all five? That's right, five:

- The word "links" in the second line below the seaside picture;
- The sentence "What about me?";
- The word "cyberspace" in the quick brown fox sentence;
- The red and white graphic in the lower left-hand corner of the page. The blue border around it matches the blue of the text links;
- The hot spot in the seaside picture. We know there's at least one link in the picture, because the cursor appears as a hand. (There may be more hot spots on the page, but we can't tell from this picture alone.)

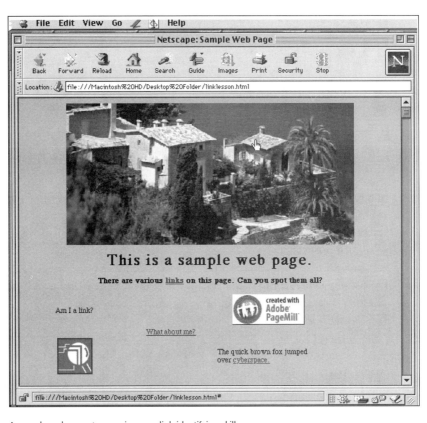

A sample web page to exercise your link identifying skills.

part

1

Getting There from Here

Now you know that a URL uniquely identifies a page and that links used as shorthand for URLs enable you to travel from page to page in the Web; but what if a link takes you someplace you don't want to go? Missing page messages take several forms, such as URL 404, Object not on this server, Missing Object, Page not Found, but they all lead to the same place—a dead end. The page specified by the link or URL no longer exists. There are many reasons for missing pages. You may have entered the URL incorrectly. Every character must be precise and no spaces are allowed. More than likely, though, especially if you arrived here via a link, the page you're after has been moved or removed. Remember, anybody can create a link to any page. In the spirit of the Internet, there are no forms to fill out, no procedures to follow. That's the good news. The bad news is that the owner of a page is under no

A missing page message, an all too common road hazard on the information superhighway.

obligation to inform the owners of links pointing to it that the page location has changed. In fact, there's no way for the page owner to even know about all the links to her page. Yes, the Internet's spirit of independence proves frustrating sometimes, but you'll find these small inconveniences are a cheap price to pay for the benefits you receive. Philosophy aside, though, we're still stuck on a page of no interest to us. The best strategy is to back up and try another approach.

Every time you click on the **Back** button, you return to the previous page you visited. That's because your browser keeps track of the pages you visit and the order in which you visit them. The **Back** icon, and its counterpart, the **Forward** icon, allow you to retrace the steps, forward and backward, of your cyberpath. Sometimes you may want to move two, three, or a dozen pages at once. Although you can click the **Back** or **Forward** icons multiple times, Web browsers offer an easier navigation shortcut. If you use Netscape, clicking on the **Go** menu in the menu bar displays a list of your most recently visited pages, in the order you've been there. Unlike the **Back** or **Forward** icons, you can select any page from the menu, and a single click takes you directly there. There's no need to laboriously move one page a time. If you use Internet Explorer, you can click on the **History** button in the Explorer bar to see a list of links you visited in previous days and weeks, or press the arrow at the end of the Address bar to see previously visited links.

Quick Check

As a quick review, here's what we know about navigating the Web so far:

- Enter a URL directly into the Location field;
- Click on a link;
- Use the **Back** or **Forward** icons;
- Select a page from the **Go** menu.

You Can Go Home (and to Other Pages) Again

How do we return to a page hours, days, or even months later? One way is to write down the URLs of every page we may want to revisit. There's got to be a better way, and there is: We call them bookmarks (on Netscape Communicator) or favorites (on Microsoft Internet Explorer).

Like their print book namesakes, Web bookmarks (and favorites) flag specific Web pages. Selecting an item from the **Bookmark/Favorites** menu, like selecting an item from the **Go** menu, is the equivalent of entering a URL into the **Location** field of your browser, except that items in the **Bookmark/Favorites** menu are ones you've added yourself and represent pages visited over many surfing experiences, not just the most recent one.

To select a page from your bookmark list, pull down the **Bookmark/Favorites** menu and click on the desired entry. To save a favorite page location, use the Add feature available in both browsers. In Netscape Communicator, clicking on the **Add Bookmark** command makes a bookmark entry for the current page. **Add to Favorites** performs the same function in Microsoft Internet Explorer. Clicking this feature adds the location of the current page to your **Bookmark/Favorites** menu.

A cautionary note is in order here. Your bookmark or favorites list physically exists only on your personal computer, which means that if you connect to the Internet on a different computer, your list won't be available. If you routinely connect to the Internet from a computer lab, for example, get ready to carry the URLs for your favorite Web sites in your notebook or your head.

part

1

Searching and Search Engines

Returning to our cable television analogy, you may recall that we conveniently glossed over the question of how we selected a starting channel in the first place. With a million TV channels, or several million Web pages, we can't depend solely on luck guiding us to something interesting.

On the Web, we solve the problem with specialized computer programs called *search engines* that crawl through the Web, page by page, cataloging its contents. As different software designers developed search strategies, entrepreneurs established Web sites where any user could find pages containing particular words and phrases. Today, Web sites such as Yahoo!, AltaVista, Excite, WebCrawler, and HotBot offer you a "front door" to the Internet that begins with a search for content of interest.

The URLs for some popular search sites are:

Excite	`www.excite.com`
Yahoo!	`www.yahoo.com`
AltaVista	`www.altavista.digital.com`
WebCrawler	`www.webcrawler.com`
MetaCrawler	`www.metacrawler.com`
Infoseek	`www.infoseek.com`
HotBot	`www.hotbot.com`

Internet Gold Is Where You Find It

Let's perform a simple search using HotBot to find information about the history of the Internet.

part

1

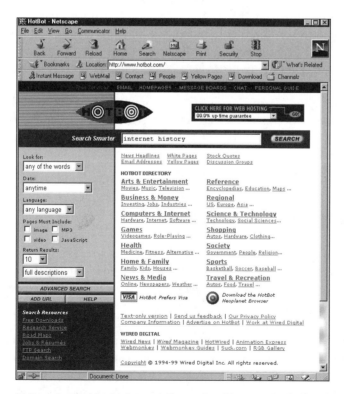

We'll start by searching for the words "internet" or "history." By looking for "any of the words," the search will return pages on which either "internet" or "history" or both appear.

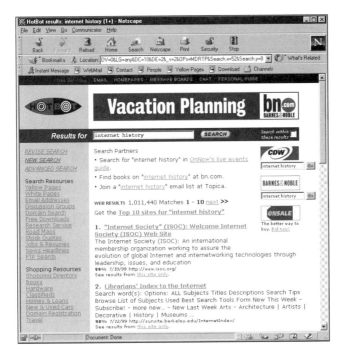

Our search returned 1,011,440 matches or *hits*. By viewing the percentage number in the last line of each summary, you will be able to see the "quality" of the match, which is usually related to the number of times the search word(s) appears on the page.

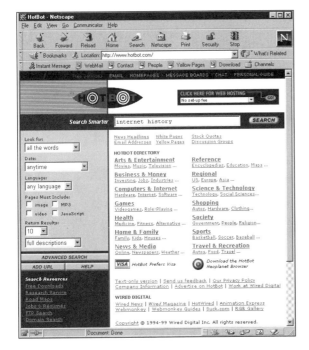

We can conduct the same search, but this time look for "all the words." The search will return hits when both "internet" and "history" appear on the same page, in any order, and not necessarily next to each other.

The search is narrowed down somewhat, but it is still not providing us with the information we need.

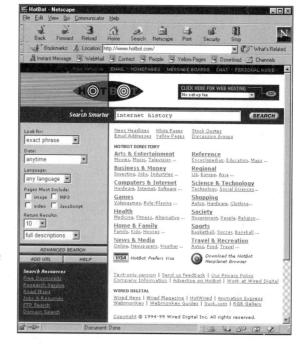

When we search for the exact phrase "internet history," which means those two words in exactly that order, with no intervening words, we're down to about 6,000 hits (still a substantial number).

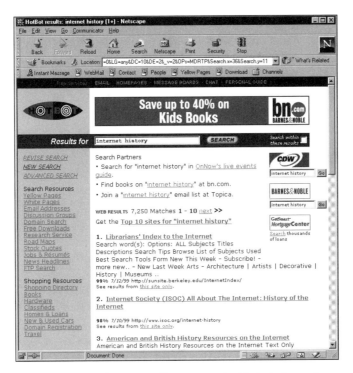

Now the first hits may be more specific. However, other hits in the list may have nothing to do with the history of the Internet. Hits happen. No search engine is 100 percent accurate 100 percent of the time. Spurious search results are the serendipity of the Internet. Look at them as an opportunity to explore something new.

Out of curiosity, let's try our history of the Internet search using a different search engine. When we search for the phrase "history of the internet" using WebCrawler, the quotation marks serve the same purpose as selecting "the exact phrase" option in Hotbot. The WebCrawler search only finds a few hundred hits. Some are the same as those found using HotBot, some are different. Different searching strategies and software algorithms make using more than one search engine a must for serious researchers.

The major search engines conveniently provide you with tips to help you get the most out of their searches. These include ways to use AND and OR to narrow down searches, and ways to use NOT to eliminate unwanted hits.

Each search engine also uses a slightly different approach to cataloging the Web, so at different sites your results might vary. Often, one search engine provides better results (more relevant hits) in your areas of interest; sometimes, the wise strategy is to provide the same input to several different engines. No one search engine does a perfect job all the time, so experience will dictate the one that's most valuable for you.

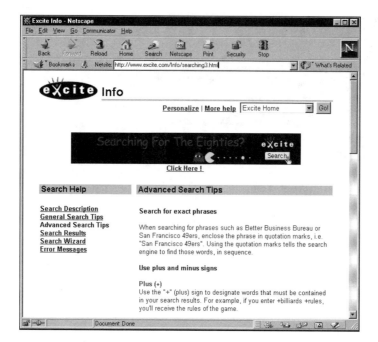

You'll find search tip pages like this at all the major search engine sites.

Quick Check

Let's review our searching strategies:

- Visit one of the search engine sites;
- Enter key words or phrases that best describe the search criteria;
- Narrow the search if necessary by using options such as "all the words" or "the exact phrase." On some search engines, you may use the word "and" or the symbol "|" to indicate words that all must appear on a page;
- Try using the same criteria with different search engines.

How Not to Come Down with a Virus

Downloading files from the Internet allows less responsible Net citizens to unleash onto your computer viruses, worms, and Trojan horses, all dangerous programs that fool you into thinking they're doing one thing while they're actually erasing your hard disk or performing some other undesirable task. Protection is your responsibility.

One way to reduce the risk of contracting a virus is to download software from reliable sites. Corporations such as Microsoft and Apple take care to make sure downloadable software is virus free. So do most institutions that provide software downloads as a public service (such as the Stanford University archives of Macintosh software). Be especially careful of programs you find on someone's home page. If you're not sure about safe download sources, ask around in a newsgroup (discussed shortly), talk to friends, or check with the information technology center on campus.

You can also buy and use a reliable virus program. Norton, Symantec, and Dr. Solomon all sell first-rate programs for the Mac and PC. You can update these programs right from the Internet so they'll detect the most current viruses. Most of the time, these programs can disinfect files/documents on your disk that contain viruses. Crude as it may sound, downloading programs from the Internet without using a virus check is like having unprotected sex with a stranger. While downloading software may not be life threatening, imagine the consequences if your entire hard disk, including all your course work and software, is totally obliterated. It won't leave you feeling very good.

part

1

If you'd like some entertaining practice sharpening your Web searching skills, point your browser to <www.internettreasurehunt.com>, follow the directions, and you're on your way to becoming an Internet researcher extraordinaire.

The (E)mail Goes Through

Email was one of the first applications created for the Internet by its designers, who sought a method of communicating with each other directly from their keyboards. Your electronic Internet mailbox is to email what a post office box is to "snail mail" (the name Net citizens apply to ordinary, hand-delivered mail). This mailbox resides on the computer of your Internet Service Provider (ISP). That's the organization providing you with your Internet account. Most of the time your ISP will be your school; but, you may contract with one of the commercial providers, such as America Online, Mindspring, Microsoft Network, Earthlink, or AT&T. The Internet doesn't deliver a message to your door but instead leaves it in a conveniently accessible place (your mailbox) in the post office (the computer of your ISP), until you retrieve the mail using your combination (password).

part

1

If you currently have computer access to the Internet, your school or ISP assigned you a *user name* (also called a user id, account name, or account number). This user name may be your first name, your first initial and the first few characters of your last name, or some strange combination of numbers and letters only a computer could love. An email address is a combination of your user name and the unique address of the computer through which you access your email, like this:

```
username@computername.edu
```

The three letters after the dot, in this case "edu," identify the top level "domain." There are six common domain categories in use: edu (educational), com (commercial), org (organization), net (network), mil (military), and gov (government). The symbol "@"—called the "at" sign in typewriter days—serves two purposes: For computers, it provides a neat, clean separation between your user name and the computer name; for people, it makes Internet addresses more pronounceable. Your address is read: user name "at" computer name "dot" e-d-u. Suppose your Internet user name is "a4736g" and your ISP is Allyn & Bacon, the publisher of this book. Your email address might look like

```
a4736g@abacon.com
```

and you would tell people your email address is "ay-four-seven-three-six-gee at ay bacon dot com."

We Don't Just Handle Your Email, We're Also a Client

You use email with the aid of special programs called *mail clients*. As with search engines, mail clients have the same set of core features, but your access to these features varies with the type of program. On both the PC and the Mac, Netscape Communicator and Microsoft Internet Explorer give you access to mail clients while you're plugged into the Web. That way you can pick up and send mail while you're surfing the Web.

The basic email service functions are creating and sending mail, reading mail, replying to mail, and forwarding mail. First we'll examine the process of sending and reading mail, and then we'll discuss how to set up your programs so that your messages arrive safely.

Let's look at a typical mail client screen, in this case from Netscape Communicator 4.6. You reach this screen by choosing **Messenger** from under the **Communicator** menu. To send a message from scratch, choose the **New Msg** button to create a blank message form, which has fields for the recipient's address and the subject, and a window for the text of the message.

Fill in the recipient's address in the "To" field, just above the arrow. Use your own address. We'll send email to ourselves and use the same

part

1

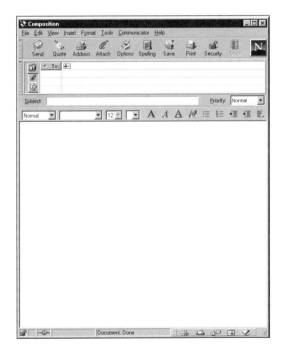

New message form, with fields for recipient's address and the subject, and a window for the text of the message.

message to practice sending email and reading it as well; then we'll know if your messages come out as expected.

Click in the "Subject" field and enter a word or phrase that generally describes the topic of the message. Since we're doing this for the first time, let's type "Maiden Email Voyage."

Now click anywhere in the text window and enter your message. Let's say "Hi. Thanks for guiding me through sending my first email." You'll find that the mail client works here like a word processing program, which means you can insert and delete words and characters and highlight text.

Now click the **Send** button on the Navigation toolbar. You've just created and sent your first email message. In most systems, it takes a few seconds to a few minutes for a message to yourself to reach your mailbox, so you might want to take a short break before continuing. When you're ready to proceed, close the **Composition** window and click the **Get Msg** button.

What Goes Around Comes Around

Now let's grab hold of the message you just sent to yourself. When retrieving mail, most mail clients display a window showing the messages in your mailbox telling you how many new messages have been added.

If you've never used your email before, chances are your message window is empty, or contains only one or two messages (usually official messages from the ISP) besides the one you sent to yourself. The message to yourself should be accompanied by an indicator of some sort—a colored mark, the letter N—indicating it's a new message. In Netscape Communicator, as in other mail clients, you also get to see the date of the message, who sent it, and the information you entered in the subject line. The Subject field lets you scan your messages and determine which ones you want to look at first.

The summary of received messages tells you everything you need to know about a message except what's in it. Click anywhere in the line to see the contents in the message window. Click on the message from yourself and you'll see the contents of the message displayed in a window. The information at the top—To, From, Subject, and so forth—is called the *header*. Depending on your system, you may also see some cryptic lines with terms such as X-Mailer, received by, and id number. Most of the time, there's nothing in this part of the header of interest, so just skip over it for now.

Moving Forward

The contents, or text, of your message can be cut and pasted just like any other text document. If you and a classmate are working on a project together, your partner can write part of a paper and email it to you, and you can copy the text from your email message and paste it into your word processing program.

What if there are three partners in this project? One partner sends you a draft of the paper for you to review. You like it and want to send it on to your other partner. The **Forward** feature lets you send the message intact, so you don't have to cut and paste it into a new message window. To forward a message, highlight it in the **Inbox** (top) and click the **Forward** icon. Enter the recipient's address in the "To" field of the message window. Note that the subject of the message is "Fwd:" followed by the subject of the original message. Use the text window to add your comments ahead of the original message.

A Chance to Reply

part

1

Email is not a one-way message system. Let's walk through a reply to a message from a correspondent named Elliot. Highlight the message in your **Inbox** again and this time click on the **Reply** icon. Depending on which program you're using, you'll see that each line in the message is preceded by either a vertical bar or a right angle bracket (>).

Note the "To" and "Subject" fields are filled in automatically with the address of the sender and the original subject preceded by "Re:". In Internet terminology, the message has been *quoted*. The vertical bar or > is used to indicate lines not written by you but by someone else (in this case, the message's original author). Why bother? Because this feature allows you to reply without retyping the parts of the message you're responding to. Because your typing isn't quoted, your answers stand out from the original message. Netscape Communicator 4.6 adds some blank lines above and below your comments, a good practice for you if your mail client doesn't do this automatically.

Welcome to the Internet, Miss Manners

While we're on the subject of email, here are some *netiquette* (net etiquette) tips.

■ When you send email to someone, even someone who knows you well, all they have to look at are your words—there's no body language attached. That means there's no smile, no twinkle in the eye, no raised eyebrow; and especially, there's no tone of voice. What you write is open to interpretation and your recipient has nothing to guide him or her. You may understand the context of a remark, but will your reader? If you have any doubts about how your message will be interpreted, you might want to tack on an *emoticon* to your message. An emoticon is a face created out of keyboard characters. For example, there's the happy Smiley :-) (you have to look at it sideways . . . the parenthesis is its mouth), the frowning Smiley :-((Frownie?), the winking Smiley ;-), and so forth. Smileys are the body language of the Internet. Use them to put remarks in context. "Great," in response to a friend's suggestion means you like the idea. "Great :-(" changes the meaning to one of disappointment or sarcasm. (Want a complete list of emoticons? Try using "emoticon" as a key word for a Web search.)

■ Keep email messages on target. One of the benefits of email is its speed. Reading through lengthy messages leaves the reader wondering when you'll get to the point.

■ Email's speed carries with it a certain responsibility. Its ease of use and the way a messages seems to cry out for an answer both encourage quick responses, but quick doesn't necessarily mean thoughtful. Once you hit the **Send** icon, that message is gone. There's no recall button. Think before you write, lest you feel the wrath of the modern-day version of your parents' adage: Answer in haste, repent at leisure.

Keeping Things to Yourself

Here's another tip cum cautionary note, this one about Web security. Just as you take care to protect your wallet or purse while walking down a crowded street, it's only good practice to exercise caution with information you'd like to keep (relatively) private. Information you pass around the Internet is stored on, or passed along by, computers that are accessible to others. Although computer system administrators take great care to insure the security of this information, no scheme is completely infallible. Here are some security tips:

- Exercise care when sending sensitive information such as credit card numbers, passwords, even telephone numbers and addresses in plain email. Your email message may pass through four or five computers en route to its destination, and at any of these points, it can be intercepted and read by someone other than the recipient.

- Send personal information over the Web only if the page is secure. Web browsers automatically encrypt information on secure pages, and the information can only be unscrambled at the Web site that created the secure page. You can tell if a page is secure by checking the status bar at the bottom of your browser's window for an icon of a closed lock.

- Remember that any files you store on your ISP's computer are accessible to unscrupulous hackers.

- Protect your password. Many Web client programs, such as mail clients, have your password for you. That means anyone with physical access to your computer can read your email. With a few simple tools, someone can even steal your password. Never leave your password on a lab computer. (Make sure the **Remember Password** or **Save Password** box is unchecked in any application that asks for your password.)

part

1

The closed lock icon in the lower left-hand corner of your browser window indicates a "secure" Web page.

An Audience Far Wider Than You Imagine

Remember that the Web in particular and the Internet in general are communications mediums with a far-reaching audience, and placing information on the Internet is tantamount to publishing it. Certainly, the contents of any message or page you post become public information, but in a newsgroup (an electronic bulletin board), your email address also becomes public knowledge. On a Web page, posting a photo of your favorite music group can violate the photographer's copyright, just as if you published the image in a magazine. Use common sense about posting information you or someone else expects to remain private; and, remember, information on the Web can and will be read by people with different tastes and sensitivities. The Web tends to be self-censoring, so be prepared to handle feedback, both good and bad.

A Discussion of Lists

There's no reason you can't use email to create a discussion group. You pose a question, for example, by sending an email message to everyone in the group. Somebody answers and sends the answer to everyone else on the list, and so on.

At least, that's the theory.

In practice, this is what often happens. As people join and leave the group, you and the rest of your group are consumed with updating your lists, adding new names and deleting old ones. As new people join, their addresses may not make it onto the lists of all the members of the group, so different participants get different messages. The work of administering the lists becomes worse than any value anyone can get out of the group, and so it quickly dissolves.

Generally, you're better off letting the computer handle discussion group administration. A *list server* is a program for administering emailing lists. It automatically adds and deletes list members and handles the distribution of messages.

part

1

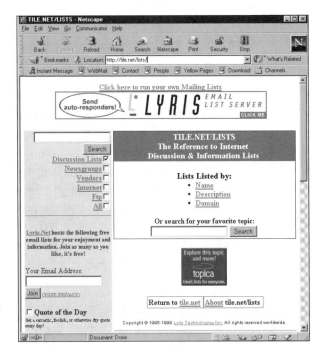

Tile.Net offfers shortcuts to working your way through the Internet's maze of discussion lists.

Thousands of mailing lists have already been formed by users with common interests. You may find mailing lists for celebrities, organizations, political interests, occupations, and hobbies. Your instructor may establish a mailing list for your course.

Groups come in several different flavors. Some are extremely active. You can receive as many as forty or more email messages a day. Other lists may send you a message a month. One-way lists, such as printed newsletters, do not distribute your reply to any other subscriber. Some lists distribute replies to everyone. These lists include mediated lists, in which an "editor" reviews each reply for suitability (relevance, tone, use of language) before distributing the message, and unmediated lists, in which each subscriber's response is automatically distributed to all the other subscribers with no restrictions except those dictated by decency and common sense, though these qualities may not always be obvious from reading the messages.

Get on a List Online

You join in the discussion by subscribing to a list, which is as straight-forward as sending email. You need to know only two items: the name of the list and the address of the list server program handling subscriptions. To join a list, send a **Subscribe** message to the list server address. The message must contain the letters "Sub," the name of the list, and your name (your real name, not your user name), all on one line. *And that's all.* This message will be read by a computer program that looks for these items only. At the very best, other comments in the message will be ignored. At the very worst, your entire message will be ignored, and so will you.

Within a few hours to a day after subscribing, the list server will automatically send you a confirmation email message, including instructions for sending messages, finding out information about the list and its members, and canceling your subscription. Save this message for future reference. That way, if you do decide to leave the list, you won't have to circulate a message to the members asking how to unsubscribe, and you won't have to wade through fifty replies all relaying the same information you received when you joined.

Soon after your confirmation message appears in your mailbox, and depending on the activity level of the list, you'll begin receiving email messages. New list subscribers customarily wait a while before joining the discussion. After all, you're electronically strolling into a room full of strangers; it's only fair to see what topics are being discussed before

part

1

wading in with your own opinions. Otherwise, you're like the bore at the party who elbows his way into a conversation with "But enough about you, let's talk about me." You'll also want to avoid the faux pas of posting a long missive on a topic that subscribers spent the preceding three weeks thrashing out. Observe the list for a while, understand its tone and feel, what topics are of interest to others and what areas are taboo. Also, look for personalities. Who's the most vociferous? Who writes very little but responds thoughtfully? Who's the most flexible? The most rigid? Most of all, keep in mind that there are far more observers than participants. What you write may be read by 10 or 100 times more people than those whose names show up in the daily messages.

When you reply to a message, you reply to the list server address, not to the address of the sender (unless you intend for your communication to remain private). The list server program takes care of distributing your message listwide. Use the address in the "Reply To" field of the message. Most mail clients automatically use this address when you select the **Reply** command. Some may ask if you want to use the reply address (say yes). Some lists will send a copy of your reply to you so you know your message is online. Others don't send the author a copy, relying on your faith in the infallibility of computers.

In the words of those famous late night television commercials, you can cancel your subscription at any time. Simply send a message to the address you used to subscribe (which you'll find on that confirmation message you saved for reference), with "Unsub," followed on the same line by the name of the list. For example, to leave a list named "WRITER-L," you would send:

```
Unsub WRITER-L
```

Even if you receive messages for a short while afterwards, have faith—they will disappear.

Waste Not, Want Not

List servers create an excellent forum for people with common interests to share their views; however, from the Internet standpoint, these lists are terribly wasteful. First of all, if there are one thousand subscribers to a list, every message must be copied one thousand times and distributed over the Internet. If there are forty replies a day, this one list creates forty thousand email messages. Ten such lists mean almost a half million messages, most of which are identical, flying around the Net.

Another wasteful aspect of list servers is the way in which messages are answered. The messages in your mailbox on any given day represent a combination of new topics and responses to previous messages. But where are these previous messages? If you saved them, they're in your email mailbox taking up disk space. If you haven't saved them, you have nothing to compare the response to. What if a particular message touches off a chain of responses, with subscribers referring not only to the source message but to responses as well? It sounds like the only safe strategy is to save every message from the list, a suggestion as absurd as it is impractical.

What we really need is something closer to a bulletin board than a mailing list. On a bulletin board, messages are posted once. Similar notices wind up clustered together. Everyone comes to the same place to read or post messages.

And Now the News(group)

part
1

The Internet equivalent of the bulletin board is the Usenet or newsgroup area. Usenet messages are copied only once for each ISP supporting the newsgroup. If there are one thousand students on your campus reading the same newsgroup message, there need only be one copy of the message stored on your school's computer.

Categorizing a World of Information

Newsgroups are categorized by topics, with topics broken down into subtopics and sub-subtopics. For example, you'll find newsgroups devoted to computers, hobbies, science, social issues, and "alternatives." Newsgroups in this last category cover a wide range of topics that may not appeal to the mainstream. Also in this category are beginning newsgroups.

Usenet names are amalgams of their topics and subtopics, separated by dots. If you were interested in a newsgroup dealing with, say, music, you might start with rec.music and move down to rec.music.radiohead, or rec.music.techno, and so forth. The naming scheme allows you to zero in on a topic of interest.

Getting into the News(group) Business

Most of the work of reading, responding to, and posting messages is handled by a news reader client program, accessible through both Netscape Communicator and Microsoft Internet Explorer. You can not only surf the Web and handle your mail via your browser, but you can also drop into your favorite newsgroups virtually all in one operation.

Let's drop into a newsgroup. To reach groups via Netscape Communicator 4.6, go to the Communicator menu bar and select **Newsgroups.** Then, from the File menu, select **Subscribe.** A dialogue box will open that displays a list of available groups.

To subscribe to a newsgroup—that is, to tell your news reader you want to be kept up-to-date on the messages posted to a particular group—highlight the group of interest and click on **Subscribe.** Alternately, you can click in the Subscribe column to the right of the group name. The check mark in the Subscribe column means you're "in."Now, click **OK.**

part
1

The message center in Netscape Communicator displays a list of newsgroups on your subscription list. Double click on the one of current interest and your reader presents you with a list of messages posted on the group's bulletin board. Double click on a message to open its contents in a window.

Often, messages contain "Re:" in their subject lines, indicating a response to a previous message (the letters stand for "Regarding"). Many news readers maintain a *thread* for you. Threads are chains of messages and all responses to that message. These readers give you the option to read messages chronologically or to read a message followed by its responses.

When you subscribe to a newsgroup, your news reader will also keep track of the messages you've read so that it can present you with the newest (unread) ones. While older messages are still available to you, this feature guarantees that you stay up-to-date without any record keeping on your part. Subscribing to a newsgroup is free, and the subscription information resides on your computer.

Newsgroups have no way of knowing who their subscribers are, and the same caveat that applies to bookmarks applies to newsgroups. Information about your subscriptions resides physically on the personal computer you're using. If you switch computers, as in a lab, your subscription information and history of read messages are beyond your reach.

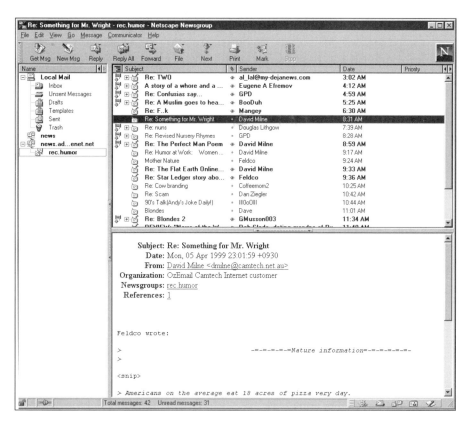

The top part of this figure shows a listing of posted messages. While not visible from this black and white reproduction, a red indicator in the Subject column marks unread messages. Double-clicking on a message opens its contents into a window shown in the bottom part of this figure. You can reply to this message via the Reply icon, or get the next message using the Next icon.

part

1

Welcome to the Internet, Miss Manners—Again

As with list servers, hang out for a while, or *lurk*, to familiarize yourself with the style, tone, and content of newsgroup messages. As you probably surmised from the names of the groups, their topics of discussion are quite narrow. One of the no-nos of newsgroups is posting messages on subjects outside the focus of the group. Posting off-topic messages, especially lengthy ones, is an excellent way to attract a flaming.

A *flame* is a brutally debasing message from one user to another. Flames are designed to hurt and offend, and often the target of the flame feels compelled to respond in kind to protect his or her self-esteem. This leads to a *flame war,* as other users take sides and wade in with flames of their own. If you find yourself the target of a flame, your best strategy is to ignore it. As with a campfire, if no one tends to the flames, they soon die out.

As mentioned earlier, posting messages to newsgroups is a modern form of publishing, and a publisher assumes certain responsibilities. You have a duty to keep your messages short and to the point. Many newsgroup visitors connect to the Internet via modems. Downloading a day's worth of long postings, especially uninteresting ones, is annoying and frustrating. Similarly, don't post the same message to multiple, related newsgroups. This is called *cross posting,* and it's a peeve of Net citizens who check into these groups. If you've ever flipped the television from channel to channel during a commercial break only to encounter the same commercial (an advertising practice called *roadblocking*), you can imagine how annoying it is to drop in on several newsgroups only to find the same messages posted to each one.

With the huge potential audience newsgroups offer, you might think you've found an excellent medium for advertising goods or services. After all, posting a few messages appears analogous to running classified ads in newspapers, only here the cost is free. There's a name for these kinds of messages—*spam.* Spam is the junk mail of the Internet, and the practice of spamming is a surefire way to attract flames. The best advice for handling spam? Don't answer it. Not only does an answer encourage the spammer, but he or she will also undoubtedly put your email address on a list and sell it to other spammers, who will flood your online mailbox with their junk.

Above all, be considerate of others. Treat them the way you'd like to be treated. Do you enjoy having your grammar or word choices corrected in front of the whole world? Do you feel comfortable when someone calls you stupid in public? Do you appreciate having your religion, ethnicity, heritage, or gender belittled in front of an audience? Respect the rights and feelings of others, if not out of simple decency then out of the sanctions your ISP may impose. Although you have every right to express an unpopular opinion or to take issue with the postings of others, most ISPs have regulations about the kinds of messages one can send via their facilities. Obscenities, threats, and spam may, at a minimum, result in your losing your Internet access privileges.

Give Your Web Browser Some Personality—Yours

Before accessing email and newsgroup functions, you need to set up or personalize your browser. If you always work on the same personal computer, this is a one-time operation that takes only a few minutes. In it, you tell your browser where to find essential computer servers, along with personal information the Internet needs to move messages for you.

- *Step 1:* Open the **Preferences** menu in Netscape or the **Internet Options** in Internet Explorer. In Netscape Communicator the Preferences menu is located under the **Edit** menu; in Microsoft Internet Explorer the Internet Options can be found under the **View** menu.

- *Step 2:* Tell the browser who you are and where to find your mail servers. Your Reply To address is typically the same as your email address, though if you have an email alias you can use it here. Microsoft Internet Explorer has slots for your mail servers in the same window. Your ISP will provide the server names and addresses. Be sure to use your user name (and not your alias) in the "Account Name" field. SMTP handles your outgoing messages, while the POP3 server routes incoming mail. Often, but not always, these server names are the same. Netscape Communicator has a separate window for server names.

- *Step 3:* Tell the browser where to find your news server. Your ISP will furnish the name of the server. Note that in Microsoft Internet Explorer, you specify a helper application to read the news. Now that most computers come with browsers already loaded onto the hard disk, you'll find that these helper applications are already set up for you.

- *Step 4:* Set your home page. For convenience, you may want your browser to start by fetching a particular page, such as your favorite search site. Or you might want to begin at your school library's home page. Enter the URL for this starting page in the home page address field. Both Netscape and Microsoft offer the option of no home page when you start up. In that case, you get a blank browser window.

Operating systems such as Mac OS 8 and Microsoft Windows 95 and 98 offer automated help in setting up your browsers for Web, mail,

part

1

and newsgroup operation. You need to know the names of the servers mentioned above, along with your user name and other details, such as the address of the domain name server (DNS) of your ISP. You should receive all this information when you open your Internet account. If not, ask for it.

Social Work and the Internet

Social workers are dedicated to the enhancement of well-being and meeting the basic human needs of all people in our society, particularly those who are vulnerable and at risk. Social workers work with and on behalf of individuals, families, groups, organizations, and communities in order to promote social justice and social change. Social workers assume a variety of roles in their work, including direct practice, community organizing, supervision, consultation, administration, advocacy, social and political action, policy development and implementation, education, and research and evaluation. Through these strategies, social workers attempt to enhance people's capacity to address their own needs as well as to promote the responsiveness of organizations, communities, and other social institutions to solving social problems and providing for human needs.

Clearly, social workers need a variety of different types of information in order to perform this multitude of tasks effectively. They need up-to-date information about populations at risk, prevalence of social problems, and causes of human suffering. They also need information about the efficacy of social interventions, descriptions of helping strategies, contacts in other social work agencies dealing with similar populations and problems, and consultation on how to implement effective programs in agency settings. Furthermore, social workers need information on federal, state, and local legislation which will affect the people with whom they work, as well as information about other sources of funding for research and demonstration programs. All of this information and more is available within a few keystrokes and mouse clicks on the Internet.

Given the wide variety of information types that social workers need, it is somewhat surprising that the social work profession is just beginning to use the Internet as a source of information for practice decision making. One explanation for this relative lack of familiarity with the "information superhighway" may be an earlier lack of emphasis on

part

1

computer literacy in social work education. In addition, as a profession dedicated in large part to working with people in poverty situations, social work professionals have, until recently, eschewed the use of personal computers for their professional practices.

Fortunately, the social work profession has begun to promote computer and Internet literacy for its members through "technology centers" at national conferences and within social work education and continuing education settings. Human service organizations, governmental agencies, and professional associations are jumping on the bandwagon, establishing World Wide Web sites to provide social workers with access to the Internet. These sites provide linkages to, among other things, empirical data, descriptions of social work interventions, contact information for other professionals working in similar settings and/or with similar populations, and information about existing policies and pending legislation which guides the implementation of social work interventions. Although it may have had a late start, the social work profession is rapidly making up for lost time in establishing a social work presence on the Internet.

As a social work student in the information age, you are in a unique position to shape the profession's use of the Internet to enhance the profession. By learning how to use the Internet now to access knowledge for practice and to communicate with social workers and others around the globe, you will be more likely than your social work predecessors to use cutting edge information in the development and implementation of your practice. As you mature in your role as a social work professional, it is likely that you will pass your knowledge of the Internet on to others, particularly to your colleagues, but perhaps also to your own social work students of the future.

part

1

Using the Internet for Social Work Practice

The social work presence on the Internet, particularly on the World Wide Web, is increasing at an exponential rate. At the time of this writing, it has been estimated that hundreds of pages relevant to the social work profession are added to the World Wide Web on a daily basis! With increasing access by social workers to the Internet, increasing popularity of Web surfing, and the ready availability of Web-authoring software, we probably can expect the number of social work-relevant Web sites to explode within the next year.

Through the Internet, social workers can access information in a matter of minutes via the personal computer on their desktops. Until a little more than a few years ago, this same information required significantly more time, long-distance telephone charges, a quantity of postage stamps, and/or a trip to a local library to access. Because libraries were often unable to keep up with pertinent information which can change on a daily basis, much of the information warehoused there was out-of-date, resulting in missing or inadequate information for social workers to make optimal practice decisions.

Social workers in isolated, rural settings or those working with rare types of problems are benefiting from Internet-based communications in the form of supervision or consultation with others with whom contact would otherwise be prohibitively expensive. With the advent of Internet-based audio–video capabilities, social workers will be able to converse in real time with other social workers. In some cases, this same communication capability will enable social workers to check in with home-bound, isolated, or rural clients who may otherwise have difficulty accessing services. Furthermore, these computer-mediated communication capabilities are already being used to facilitate distance education of social workers.

Social workers are also making use of the Internet as a communication medium. Many social work agencies and social workers in private practice have developed personal Web pages to publicize their services to other social workers and to potential consumers. Social workers use the Internet to alert others to legislative issues of relevance to social work practice and the people we serve, and many social workers use email to contact elected officials to advocate on these issues. Social workers in community development roles are beginning to use the Internet to bring together neighborhoods and interest groups. Finally, it is now more possible for social workers in geographically distant locations to collaborate in real time on topics and issues of mutual interest.

Before discussing strategies for accessing social work-relevant information on the Internet, it might be helpful to review the types of information that are available to social workers on the Net. New World Wide Web sites related to social work are established on a weekly basis. In addition to social work-specific sites, social workers make regular use of information provided by others, including allied professions, social science disciplines, advocacy organizations, and governmental agencies. Information relevant to social work practice decision making can be found on the World Wide Web, in online databases, and in document repositories located around the world. Some types of social work-related infor-

part

1

mation can be found in Usenet newsgroups, through a variety of electronic mailing lists, and even in online, real-time chat groups made possible through Internet Relay Chat (IRC) networks or, more recently, through World Wide Web-based chat programs.

Social work information on the Internet appears in a variety of contexts. Most major social work professional associations, as well as many smaller such groups, have established Web sites to provide information about the organization, contact information for key offices and people within the organization, calendar and special program updates for their membership, as well as action alerts on issues ranging from political lobbying efforts to texts of pending key legislation. These organizational sites often provide links to related Web sites, such as those established by chapters of the organization, by related organizational groups, and other Web sites and information sources thought to be useful to individuals accessing their site.

On a more local level, chapters of national associations often establish World Wide Web sites to provide information about membership activities, state-specific legislation, and links to licensing or other certifying boards within their state. These sites sometimes provide listings of social work jobs available, helping members who are seeking employment. Further, many of these local chapters have established local electronic mailing lists which provide information to their membership about local events, activities, and issues.

part

1

Many World Wide Web sites represent human service organizations or coalitions of human service organizations which serve to inform the profession and the public about the services that these agencies provide. Information describing services offered by these agencies, contact information, and information about the efficacy of interventions offered are often featured.

Advocacy organizations often present factual information about the problems they address and the populations that they serve, as well as links to governmental agencies which implement policies and fund programs for targeted groups. These governmental agencies, in turn, often provide links to government documents containing information critical to social work practice decision making.

Electronic journals relevant to social work practice are beginning to appear on the World Wide Web. These Web sites provide quality information on a timely basis for social workers, and at significantly less cost than printed journals. In time, these sites may make information available on a paid subscription basis, making the types of peer review used in print medium journals possible.

Social work educational programs housed in university settings were among the earliest groups to publish World Wide Web sites. In addition to providing information to prospective students, schools of social work are beginning to offer distance education programs using the Internet for curriculum delivery. Faculty in these academic settings have an opportunity to publicize their current research, and sometimes make available unpublished manuscripts which can be read online or downloaded for later perusal. Some university settings can be thought of as "World Wide Web supersites," presenting lists of links to myriad other social work resources.

Finding Social Work Information on the Internet

Social workers need to be able to locate relevant information quickly. Although one might think that with increasing availability of information, it is easier to find, but that is not true in the case of the Internet, because the amount of information in general is increasing exponentially! With the burgeoning availability of information relevant to social work practice on the Internet, the issue of selecting the most appropriate of the available information becomes important. How do we separate the wheat from the chaff, so to speak? Evaluation of the appropriateness of available information becomes more important when more information is accessible. Finally, social workers need to able to use the information that they find on the Internet. While the topic of knowledge utilization in general is beyond the scope of this book, social work students, in particular, need to be able to provide citations for the information they find.

Searching the Internet

There are four important steps in any search for information on the Internet. First, it is important that you define what it is that you are looking for. Are you looking for communication with others, original research, descriptions of programs, or descriptions of human problems? Different types of information are more likely to be found in some places than others, and learning about where to find which kind of information will likely save you a lot of time and effort in your search.

Second, it is important to be creative with keywords. As was discussed earlier, judicious use of keywords in your search can mean the difference between finding two million hits or two hundred, much more appropriate, hits. Sometimes, finding the right words to use in your search takes some surfing around the Web. As you read from related sites, the concepts you are searching for will become more clear, and different keywords will emerge. Using these new keywords will prove more fruitful in finding just the information you need.

Third, it is important that you select the most appropriate search tool for the task at hand. Search engines and directories are proliferating; new ones are available every month. Many people who routinely search the Internet for information like to use search indexes to begin their search for information, and then use keywords to narrow their search for more specific information. A helpful resource for understanding how to use search tools is available from the University of Indianapolis at http:// socwork.uindy.edu/links/search1.htm.

Finally, just as it is important to evaluate the social work-relevant knowledge you read in the library, it is even more crucial that you evaluate critically any information that you obtain through the Internet. Why is critical evaluation even more important here? While librarians have a limited budget with which to purchase volumes and thus must select carefully from what is available, no such filtering exists on the Net. Anyone with Internet access and a little bit of skill can publish anything they want on the World Wide Web. In other words, there's a lot of useless information out there, and it's in the profession's best interests that social workers know the difference.

part

1

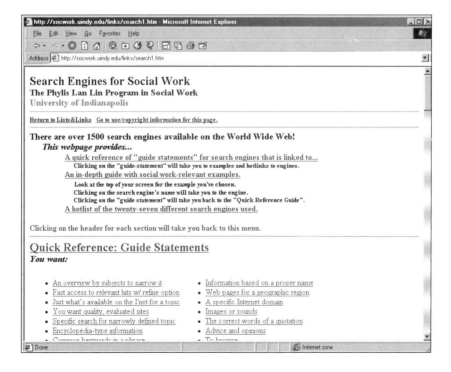

Surfing the Web for Social Work Resources

Sometimes, the most appropriate way to search the Net is not to use a search engine at all, but allow yourself some time to *surf* the net for information. Much of this section of the book will address strategies for successful surfing of the Internet for social work information.

At the beginning of a search for information, it is often the case that the concepts being researched are ill-formed and vague. Sometimes, it may even be that you don't have much knowledge about what you are looking for at all! Sometimes, although you know what you're looking for, keyword searches just don't locate enough information. When any of the above is the case, or if you simply want to learn more about social work as a profession, the answer may be to allow yourself some time to *surf* the World Wide Web.

Surfing the Web requires some time, which is often a luxury. It is easy to underestimate the amount of time it will take to find information on the Internet using the surf method rather than the more conservative search strategies outlined in the first part of this book. There are some techniques for surfing the Web that may make your surfing more efficient, however, and what follows is intended to assist you in learning these techniques.

One final caution with respect to surfing the Web is that it is easy to get lost. My own tendency is to follow links that look interesting, and to, sometime later, find myself in a completely unrelated site. Be careful! It is important to stop periodically and remind yourself of the questions you were seeking answers to when you started to surf. It is also important to remember the built-in safety mechanisms in your Web browser software. In either Netscape or Internet Explorer, use the **GO** menu to find the last page that looks like it was relevant to your search and to return there. In Part III of this book, you will find an annotated list of URLs for social work-relevant sites I have visited and found to be useful. The problem with a list like this is that, despite countless hours of work on my part, it is incomplete by the time it is printed. In addition, thousands of new pages are appearing on the Web weekly and existing pages expire, change addresses, or otherwise become obsolete.

The listed sites appear in alphabetical order by category, and the various categories of sites will be discussed below. The categories are not mutually exclusive, and someone else might have categorized them in a different way. The categories and the sites listed within these categories are meant to be illustrative of the types of information out there, rather than an assessment of the state of the Web.

Getting Your Feet Wet: The Social Work Megasites

In starting the surfing process, I often find it useful to start with the social work *megasites,* Web sites which provide lists of links to other sites, often by categories. One of the most comprehensive of these megasites is that developed by Dr. Gary Holden at New York University at http://pages.nyu.edu/~gh5/gh-w3-f.htm. This site lists literally hundreds of URLs of social work relevant Web pages.

One potential problem with a list like Dr. Holden's is that it can be overwhelming. The list can take a long time to load, and the sheer volume of resources offered can make it seem daunting. A megasite which has attempted to address this issue is the SWAN (Social Work Access Network) site sponsored by the University of South Carolina College of Social Work at http://www.sc.edu/swan. This site, in addition to organizing links by topical areas, uses buttons to take the user to different pages within the site.

Paddling Out to the Wave, Part I: Social Work Academic Sites

An important category of sites which can be helpful in starting your search efforts are sites hosted by schools of social work. Universities and colleges were, understandably, among the first to establish Web sites. In addition to telling about their programs, many schools offer links to library searches, research centers, and document repositories.

For a complete list of social work programs on the Internet, look at Gary Holden's site at http://pages.nyu.edu/~gh5/gh-w3-f.htm. The list of social work education sites in Part III of this book includes only those sites which provide more than just descriptions of their programs.

Paddling Out, Part II: Government Resources

World Wide Web sites that are sponsored by various governmental can also make for fruitful surfing, particularly if you are seeking statistical information, policy formulations, or authoritative information on a particular topic. One site which has important utility for social work is the United States Bureau of the Census at http://www.census.gov. This site provides access to U.S. Census data, and provides easy database access for users to download information by locality.

part

1

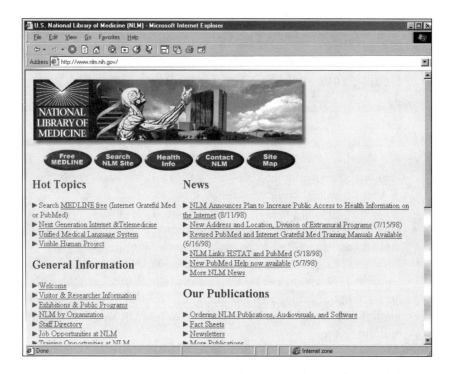

Another important resource is the National Library of Medicine at http://www.nlm.nih.gov/. This site allows users to access special publications of the library, to look at online databases and documents, and to look at sites outside the National Library through links.

Paddling Out, Part III: Professional Association Sites

Professional associations to which social workers belong often host Web sites which can be helpful resources in surfing the Web. For example, the Web site of the National Association of Social Workers at http://www.socialworkers.org/ can be a helpful resource when trying to find out about the activities of the NASW Chapter in your own state.

Paddling Out, Part IV: Electronic Journals and Newsletters

Electronic journals and newsletters are beginning to appear with increasing frequency on the World Wide Web. Sometimes these sites represent online versions of regular print media, and the information posted on the site represents selected contents of recent issues. In these cases, the information is as good as the peer review process used to select the contents of the regular journal.

Many print journals publish their tables of contents and abstracts of articles, but do not publish the text of the articles themselves on the Web. Even so, perusing the recent contents of a journal can represent an incredible savings of time over traveling to your local library to do the same thing. If you find what you are looking for, you still need to go to the library to pick up the text of the article, but you are more likely to know that what you are retrieving is worthwhile, based on your previous review.

In contrast with the above, many sites are beginning to establish journals which are entirely online. The more scholarly of these journals use peer review processes which are just as stringent as printed journals, but the advantage, of course, is that information can be published much more quickly on the Web.

Catching the Wave: Social Work Areas of Practice Sites

In addition to the kinds of sites listed above, there are thousands of World Wide Web sites which pertain to any of several areas of practice, and which may assist you with finding the information you need. In addition to using the list at the back of this book, many of the categories discussed above list sites which provide links by area of practice.

part

1

Administration Many social workers perform administrative functions within human service organizations. Social workers in these settings need to know about working with boards, volunteers, donors, and foundations. The resources available on the Internet should give these social workers a running start. For example, GuideStar at http://www.guidestar.org/ provides information on the programs and finances of more than 600,000 American nonprofit organizations, up-to-date news stories and features on philanthropy, and a forum for donors and volunteers.

Aging Social workers who work with elders will find many resources out on the Web from which to choose. Many sites have been developed for use by older adults or caregivers of older adults, and there are many professional references available as well. Some sites are designed with both audiences in mind. For example, The ALZHEIMER Page at http://www.biostat.wustl.edu/alzheimer provides links to just about

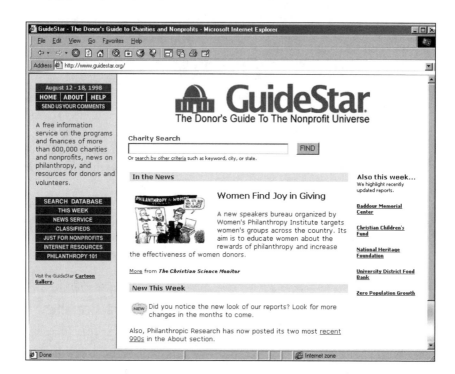

everything you'd want to know about Alzheimer's disease, and in letters so big that you won't need your glasses.

Children, Adolescents, and Families There are many Internet sites devoted to the needs of children and families. Even Disney is getting into social work issues. See their site at Family.com (http://family.disney.com/). The site provides information about family travel, home improvement projects, and parenting issues.

Clinical Social Work Practice A wide variety of information on approaches to social work direct practice are available on the Internet. One interesting resource is FreudNet: The A. A. Brill Library at http://www.interport.net/nypsan/, which provides access to information about library services and the collection, as well as general information about psychoanalysis.

Community Organization Community organizers are finding that the Web not only provides information about community organization efforts world-wide, it also can be used to build community. A particularly good link is NetAction Internet Resources at http://www.netaction.org/

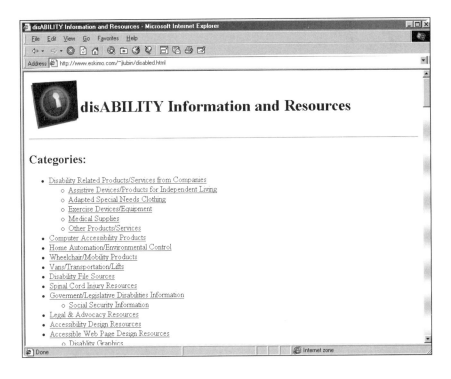

part

1

resources.html. This site lists links for virtually everything you need to know to be a community activist using the Internet.

Disabilities The wealth of information on the Internet for people with disabilities is incredible. A friend I met on the Net, who is deaf, calls the Internet "the great equalizer." Deaf people have access to the same text features as the hearing, and speech synthesis is making the Internet accessible to people with visual impairments. disABILITY Information and Resources at http://www.eskimo.com/~jlubin/disabled.html is one of the largest collections of resources pertaining to all types of disabilities.

Diversity The ease of publishing on the World Wide Web has made it possible for people of color to preserve and transmit their culture as never has been possible before. The list in the back of the book lists only a few of the many diversity resources available out on the Web.

Many of these sites have been published by individuals, rather than institutions. In this case, lack of institutional authority is not a detriment. See the African American Home Page at http://www.lainet.com/~joejones/. This site provides access to African American resources, including one of the largest collections of African American art on the

Internet. It also includes recipes, bulletin boards, library resources, and links to related sites.

Gender There are many excellent resources on the Net pertaining to gender issues. One of the most complete sites for women's issues is Feminist.Com at http://feminist.com/, which is aimed at helping women network, and educating and empowering women (and men) on issues that affect their lives.

Health Resources related to health issues are well-developed, perhaps because the medical profession has been using the World Wide Web since its inception. Med Help International at http://medhlp.netusa.net/ is dedicated to helping all who are in need find qualified medical information and support for their medical conditions and questions, regardless of their economic status or geographic location. The site offers library searches and patient support through chat resources.

HIV/AIDS Some of the best information about HIV and AIDS is available on the World Wide Web, largely because so much information is just now becoming available. One of the best resources is the Detroit Community AIDS Library (DCAL) at http://www.libraries.wayne.edu/ dcal/aids.html which serves as the gateway to HIV/AIDS Information for Detroit and Southeastern Michigan.

Housing, Hunger, and Poverty There are many resources available to social workers interested in working with the poor and the homeless. Organizations world-wide post information about the services they offer and share resources with each other.

One of the most interesting resources in this area is Real Change at http://www.realchangenews.org/, a newspaper for the homeless of Seattle, Washington.

Mental Health There is a plethora of information available on the Internet pertinent to mental health concerns. Mental Health Net at http://www.cmhc.com/ considers itself the largest, most comprehensive guide to mental health online, featuring over 6,000 individual resources. This site, winner of several awards, covers information on disorders such as depression, anxiety, panic attacks, chronic fatigue syndrome, and substance abuse, to professional resources in psychology, psychiatry and social work, journals, and self-help magazines.

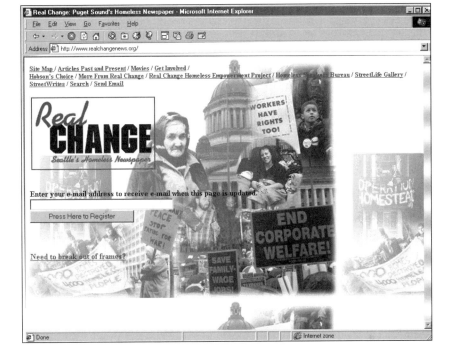

Policy Practice Many of the Internet resources related to social policy are located in the government sites and on Web sites of think tanks associated with universities. However, there are several sites which seem devoted exclusively to informing the Web-surfing public about important social policies. For example, there are numerous sites which present information about issues related to welfare reform. The Welfare Reform—Introduction page (http://www.epn.org/tcf/welfintr.html), presented by the Twentieth Century Fund, is especially impressive. This page is designed to substitute facts for myth in the important public battle over welfare reform. Contributors to the information presented on the site include Joel Handler, Professor of Law, University of California, Los Angeles; Yeheskel Hasenfeld, Professor of Social Welfare, University of California, Los Angeles; and Jack Sirica of Newsday.

Prevention Generalist social workers need more up-to-date information about prevention of social problems than is currently available. Most of the information on the Internet relates to substance abuse or family violence. One of the most comprehensive sites dedicated to prevention of child abuse is that of the Child Abuse Prevention Network at http://child.cornell.edu/. An initiative of Family Life Development Center

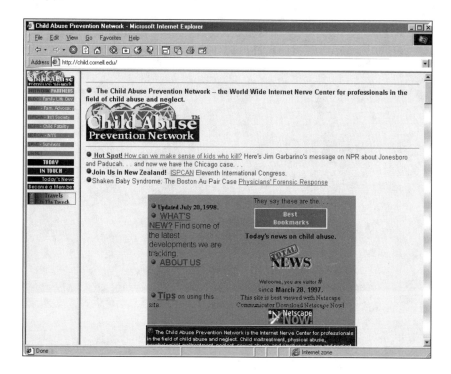

at Cornell University, the network is dedicated to enhancing internet resources for the prevention of child abuse and neglect, and reducing the negative conditions in the family and the community that lead to child maltreatment.

Research and Measurement There are many different types of resources available on the Internet related to social work research and measurement. Many of the institutions which specialize in social research have published Web sites, and many of these make available working documents about the research being conducted at their facility. For example, look at the site of the Cecil G. Sheps Center for Health Services Research at the University of North Carolina–Chapel Hill at http://www.shepscenter.unc.edu/.

Sexuality While teenagers and others are surfing the Internet looking for sexually-oriented adult sites, they may also come across valuable information that can help them by providing accurate information about issues such as sexual orientation and sexually transmitted diseases. One of the best of these sites is the Coalition for Positive Sexuality at http://www.positive.org/cps/. The Coalition for Positive Sexuality was formed to give teens the information about sexuality they need to take care of themselves and affirm their decisions about sex, sexuality, and reproductive control. They also hope to facilitate dialogue, in and out of the public schools, on condom availability and sex education. Just Say Yes, their irreverent and unabashed comprehensive sex education guide is available here.

Substance Abuse Given the pervasiveness of this problem in our society, the abundance of Internet sites devoted to substance abuse issues is not surprising. It is also not surprising that the National Clearinghouse for Alcohol and Drug Information at http://www.health.org/ provides one of the most informative sites. The site offers electronic access to searchable databases and substance abuse prevention materials that pertain to alcohol, tobacco, and drugs.

Violence Finally, there are many sites devoted to the problem of violence, particularly domestic violence, in our society. Many of these pages are devoted to providing resources for the victim of violence. One of the best violence research sites is the National Consortium on Violence Research at http://www.ncovr.heinz.cmu.edu/ (see next page). NCOVR has been created as a research and training center devoted to studying the factors contributing to inter-personal violence. The NCOVR world wide Web site is served by the H. John Heinz III School of Public Policy and Management at Carnegie Mellon University in Pittsburgh, Pennsylvania.

part

1

Riding the Wave into Shore: Social Work Mailing Lists

To discover more in-depth information about a specific social work topic, direct communication with practitioners and researchers in that practice area may be essential. Students may find it possible to communicate with the leading social work theorists by subscribing, reading, and posting to one of the many social work electronic mailing lists. The listing in Part II of this book will lead you to several Web pages describing the variety of mailing lists available. One of the best of these pages is the Social Work Listservs page maintained by the Social Work Access Network (SWAN) at http://www.sc.edu/swan/listserv.html.

When subscribing to a mailing list, be sure to save the instructions sent to you as a part of your confirmation, so that if you need to unsubscribe from the list, you know how to do so. When participating on a mailing list, it is especially important to avoid being drawn into a *flame war,* as was described earlier. Social work students should keep in mind

that the 1997 NASW Code of Ethics (http://www.naswdc.org/CODE.
HTM) stipulates that social workers should treat colleagues with respect
and avoid unwarranted criticism of colleagues in communications.

In addition to the technical guidelines for posting email and the
common-sense suggestions for netiquette discussed earlier, students may
wish to use the following checklist to review potential postings to a public mailing list before hitting the **SEND** button:

1. Do I have a good reason for sending this to the mailing list?

2. Is the message being sent to the appropriate destination (the whole
   list vs. an individual)?

3. Is the subject line descriptive of my topic?

4. Have I included just enough of any past postings that my post refers
   to so that other list members know what I am talking about?

5. Have I indicated where I agree with previous postings?

6. If I have disagreed with someone else's ideas, have I avoided a
   personal attack?

7. Have I ignored or defused anything which I consider a personal
   attack against me?

8. Does my message contribute something to the discussion? Does it
   say why I agree, give another example of the point being made, or
   in some way add to the thread? Is this post more than a "me too?"

9. Have I offered to summarize the replies to any question I asked
   earlier?

10. Have I signed the message, and included my email address in the body?

Critical Evaluation

Where Seeing Is Not Always Believing

Typical research resources, such as journal articles, books, and other
scholarly works, are reviewed by a panel of experts before being published. At the very least, any reputable publisher takes care to assure that
the author is who he or she claims to be and that the work being published represents a reasoned and informed point of view. When anyone
can post anything in a Web site or to a newsgroup, the burden of assess-

ing the relevance and accuracy of what you read falls to you. Rumors quickly grow into facts on the Internet simply because stories can spread so rapidly that the "news" seems to be everywhere. Because the Internet leaves few tracks, in no time it's impossible to tell whether you are reading independent stories or the merely same story that's been around the world two or three times. Gathering information on the Internet may be quick, but verifying the quality of information requires a serious commitment.

Approach researching via the Internet with confidence, however, and not with trepidation. You'll find it an excellent workout for your critical evaluation skills; no matter what career you pursue, employers value an employee who can think critically and independently. Critical thinking is also the basis of problem solving, another ability highly valued by the business community. So, as you research your academic projects, be assured that you're simultaneously developing lifelong expertise.

It's Okay to Be Critical of Others

The first tip for successful researching on the Internet is to always consider your source. A Web site's URL often alerts you to the sponsor of the site. CNN or MSNBC are established news organizations, and you can give the information you find at their sites the same weight you would give to their cablecasts. Likewise, major newspapers operate Web sites with articles reprinted from their daily editions or expanded stories written expressly for the Internet. On the other hand, if you're unfamiliar with the source, treat the information the way you would any new data. Look for specifics—"66 percent of all voters" as opposed to "most voters"—and for information that can be verified—a cited report in another medium or information accessible through a Web site hosted by a credible sponsor—as opposed to generalities or unverifiable claims. Look for independent paths to the same information. This can involve careful use of search engines or visits to newsgroups with both similar and opposing viewpoints. Make sure that the "independent" information you find is truly independent. In newsgroups don't discount the possibility of multiple postings, or that a posting in one group is nothing more than a quotation from a posting in another. Ways to verify independent paths include following sources (if any) back to their origins, contacting the person posting a message and asking for clarification, or checking other media for verification.

In many cases, you can use your intuition and common sense to raise your comfort level about the soundness of the information. With both list servers and newsgroups, it's possible to lurk for a while to develop a feeling for the authors of various postings. Who seems the most authoritarian, and who seems to be "speaking" from emotion or bias? Who seems to know what he or she is talking about on a regular basis? Do these people cite their sources of information (a job or affiliation perhaps)? Do they have a history of thoughtful, insightful postings, or do their postings typically contain generalities, unjustifiable claims, or flames? On Web sites, where the information feels more anonymous, there are also clues you can use to test for authenticity. Verify who's hosting the Web site. If the host or domain name is unfamiliar to you, perhaps a search engine can help you locate more information. Measure the tone and style of the writing at the site. Does it seem consistent with the education level and knowledge base necessary to write intelligently about the subject?

When offering an unorthodox point of view, good authors supply facts, figures, and quotes to buttress their positions, expecting readers to be skeptical of their claims. Knowledgeable authors on the Internet follow these same commonsense guidelines. Be suspicious of authors who expect you to agree with their points of view simply because they've published them on the Internet. In one-on-one encounters, you frequently judge the authority and knowledge of the speaker using criteria you'd be hard pressed to explain. Use your sense of intuition on the Internet, too.

As a researcher (and as a human being), the job of critical thinking requires a combination of healthy skepticism and rabid curiosity. Newsgroups and Web sites tend to focus narrowly on single issues (newsgroups more so than Web sites). Don't expect to find a torrent of opposing views on newsgroup postings; their very nature and reason for existence dampens free-ranging discussions. A newsgroup on *The X-Files* might argue about whether extraterrestrials exist but not whether the program is the premier television show on the air today. Such a discussion would run counter to the purposes of the newsgroup and would be a violation of netiquette. Anyone posting such a message would be flamed, embarrassed, ignored, or otherwise driven away. Your research responsibilities include searching for opposing views by visiting a variety of newsgroups and Web sites. A help here is to fall back on the familiar questions of journalism: who, what, when, where, and why.

■ **Who** else might speak knowledgeably on this subject? Enter that person's name into a search engine. You might be surprised to find whose work is represented on the Web. (For fun, one of the authors entered the name of a rock-and-roll New York radio disk jockey into MetaCrawler and was amazed to find several pages devoted to the DJ, including sound clips of broadcasts dating back to the sixties, along with a history of his theme song.)

■ **What** event might shed more information on your topic? Is there a group or organization that represents your topic? Do they hold an annual conference? Are synopses of presentations posted on the sponsoring organization's Web site?

■ **When** do events happen? Annual meetings or seasonal occurrences can help you isolate newsgroup postings of interest.

■ **Where** might you find this information? If you're searching for information on wines, for example, check to see if major wine-producing regions, such as the Napa Valley in California or the Rhine Valley in Germany, sponsor Web sites. These may point you to organizations or information that don't show up in other searches. Remember, Web search engines are fallible; they don't find every site you need.

■ **Why** is the information you're searching for important? The answer to this question can lead you to related fields. New drugs, for example, are important not only to victims of diseases but to drug companies and the FDA as well.

part

1

Approach assertions you read from a skeptic's point of view. See if they stand up to critical evaluation or if you're merely emotionally attached to them. Imagine "What if . . . ?" or "What about . . . ?" scenarios that may disprove or at least call into question what you're reading. Try following each assertion you pull from the Internet with the phrase, "On the other hand. . . ." Because you can't leave the sentence hanging, you'll be forced to finish it, and this will help get you into the habit of critically examining information.

These are, of course, the same techniques critical thinkers have employed for centuries, only now you are equipped with more powerful search tools than past researchers may have ever imagined. In the time it took your antecedents to formulate their questions, you can search dozens of potential information sources. You belong to the first generation of college students to enjoy both quantity and quality in its research, along with a wider perspective on issues and the ability to form personal opinions after reasoning from a much wider knowledge base. Certainly, the potential exists for the Internet to grind out a generation of intellectual robots, "thinkers" who don't think but who regurgitate information from many sources. Technology always has its good and bad aspects. However, we also have the potential to become some of the most well-informed thinkers in the history of the world, thinkers who are not only articulate but confident that their opinions have been distilled from a range of views, processed by their own personalities, beliefs, and biases. This is one of the aspects of the Internet that makes this era such an exciting combination of humanism and technology.

^{part}

1

part

Web Activities
for Social Work

Using Usenet Newsgroups

Until a couple of years ago, Usenet newsgroups represented one of the best ways to learn about a subject area. Because of the increase in Internet traffic over the past two years, and also because of inappropriate use of Usenet to advertise commercial and often shady enterprises, it has become somewhat less useful. Still, social work students may find Usenet to be a relatively easy way to learn information about a given subject area.

Exercise

Go to the Social Work Access Network (SWAN) site at **http://www.sc. edu/swan** and click on the **SW Topics List** link on the left side of the page. Then, under *Resources,* on the left side of the page, click on the **Newsgroups** button. Click on one of the newsgroups listed (you may need to try a few before you find one your service carries). Read some of the topics available.

- What did you learn about this topic that you didn't already know?
- Are newsgroups going to provide you with authoritative information? If not, why not?

Searching the Web for Social Work Information

Earlier, you read about how to use Internet indexes and search engines to find information. Now you can try out some of the strategies you learned with a topic area of choice.

Exercise

Select a general topic area of professional interest to you, for example, "substance abuse." Go to the University of Indianapolis site at **http://socwork.uindy.edu/links/search1.htm** and work with the information presented there about using search engines on the Web. Follow the *Quick Reference: Guide Statements* Exercise, and then the *In-Depth Guide*, using their suggestions for search engines to try first with your topic.

■ What did you learn about this topic that you didn't already know?
■ Are search engines on the Web going to help you find authoritative information? How easy was it to find what you wanted?

part

2

Surfing the Web for Social Work Information

Surfing the Web can be one of the most rewarding strategies for finding information, but you have to remain disciplined, and try not to get lost. To beat the metaphor almost to a pulp, it's easy to find yourself bobbing in the waves with the baby sea lions and the sharks if you don't keep your information objectives in mind while you are surfing.

USING SOCIAL WORK ACADEMIC SITES

Exercise

Go to the Columbia University site at **http://www.cc.columbia.edu/cu/ssw/**. Click on the **Library** button on the left, the <u>Online Resources for Social Work Research</u> link, the <u>E-Books and Journals</u> link on the left side of the page, and then examine the list of journals in Part 2. Imagine

part

2

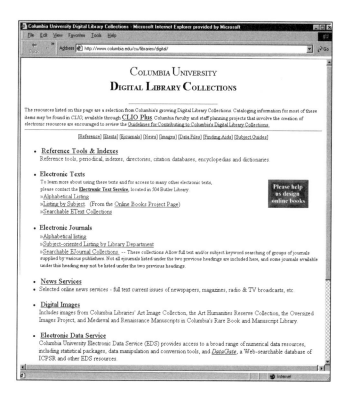

being able to do some of your suggested reading without leaving the comfort of your computer! Now, select one of the listed journals to read.

■ What happened when you tried to read from this journal? Why do you think this happened? Does your library provide such a service?

USING GOVERNMENT RESOURCES

Exercise

Go to the National Library of Medicine at **http://www.nlm.nih.gov/** and click on HIV/AIDS Resources under Special Information Programs. Click on Publications, and then on Guide to NIH HIV/AIDS Information Services. This will take you to the latest information the U.S. government has published on the topic of HIV/AIDS.

■ How authoritative is the information presented on this site?

■ How might you use information from the National Library of Medicine for your professional practice?

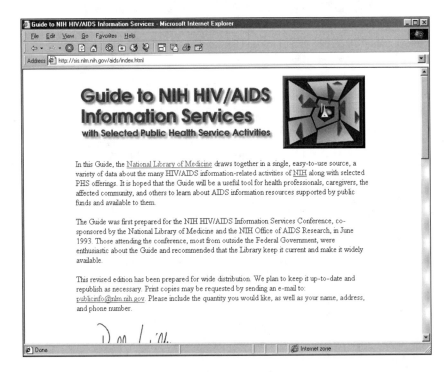

part

2

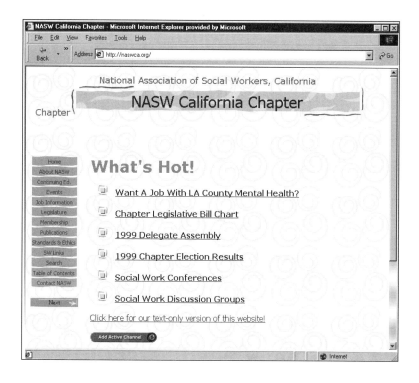

USING PROFESSIONAL ASSOCIATION SITES

Exercise

Visit the National Association of Social Workers (NASW) site at **http://www.socialworkers.org/** and click on the **Contact Chapters** button at the top of the page. Does your state chapter of NASW have email? Do they have a Web site of their own? Visit the California Chapter of NASW at **http://naswca.org.**

■ How do you think that this site will be used by the chapter membership? What aspects of the site do you think will be most helpful to social workers?

USING ELECTRONIC JOURNALS AND NEWSLETTERS

Exercise

Go to Alcohol Alerts at **http://silk.nih.gov/silk/niaaa1/publication/ alalerts.htm.** This is a quarterly bulletin of the National Institute on Alcohol Abuse and Alcoholism that disseminates important research

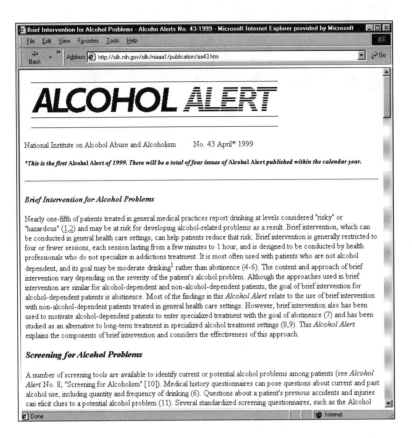

ALCOHOL ALERT

National Institute on Alcohol Abuse and Alcoholism   No. 43 April* 1999

This is the first Alcohol Alert of 1999. There will be a total of four issues of Alcohol Alert published within the calendar year.

Brief Intervention for Alcohol Problems

Nearly one-fifth of patients treated in general medical practices report drinking at levels considered "risky" or "hazardous" (1,2) and may be at risk for developing alcohol-related problems as a result. Brief intervention, which can be conducted in general health care settings, can help patients reduce that risk. Brief intervention is generally restricted to four or fewer sessions, each session lasting from a few minutes to 1 hour, and is designed to be conducted by health professionals who do not specialize in addictions treatment. It is most often used with patients who are not alcohol dependent, and its goal may be moderate drinking[1] rather than abstinence (4-6). The content and approach of brief intervention vary depending on the severity of the patient's alcohol problem. Although the approaches used in brief intervention are similar for alcohol-dependent and non-alcohol-dependent patients, the goal of brief intervention for alcohol-dependent patients is abstinence. Most of the findings in this *Alcohol Alert* relate to the use of brief intervention with non-alcohol-dependent patients treated in general health care settings. However, brief intervention also has been used to motivate alcohol-dependent patients to enter specialized treatment with the goal of abstinence (7) and has been studied as an alternative to long-term treatment in specialized alcohol treatment settings (8,9). This *Alcohol Alert* explains the components of brief intervention and considers the effectiveness of this approach.

Screening for Alcohol Problems

A number of screening tools are available to identify current or potential alcohol problems among patients (see *Alcohol Alert* No. 8, "Screening for Alcoholism" [10]). Medical history questionnaires can pose questions about current and past alcohol use, including quantity and frequency of drinking (6). Questions about a patient's previous accidents and injuries can elicit clues to a potential alcohol problem (11). Several standardized screening questionnaires, such as the Alcohol

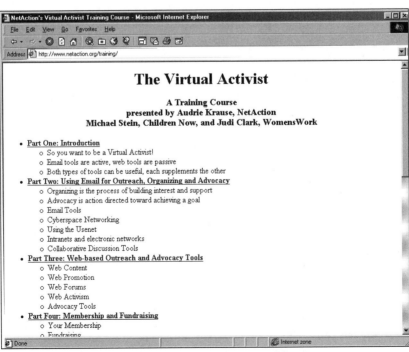

The Virtual Activist

A Training Course
presented by Audrie Krause, NetAction
Michael Stein, Children Now, and Judi Clark, WomensWork

- **Part One: Introduction**
  - So you want to be a Virtual Activist!
  - Email tools are active, web tools are passive
  - Both types of tools can be useful, each supplements the other
- **Part Two: Using Email for Outreach, Organizing and Advocacy**
  - Organizing is the process of building interest and support
  - Advocacy is action directed toward achieving a goal
  - Email Tools
  - Cyberspace Networking
  - Using the Usenet
  - Intranets and electronic networks
  - Collaborative Discussion Tools
- **Part Three: Web-based Outreach and Advocacy Tools**
  - Web Content
  - Web Promotion
  - Web Forums
  - Web Activism
  - Advocacy Tools
- **Part Four: Membership and Fundraising**
  - Your Membership
  - Fundraising

findings on a single aspect of alcohol abuse and alcoholism. Notice that you can get free copies of these bulletins by filling out the form on the page. Select a topic of interest to you and click on the link.

■ How authoritative is this information?

■ How useful would this information be for writing a paper on a related topic?

USING SOCIAL WORK AREAS OF PRACTICE SITES

Exercise

Go to Neighborhoods Online at **http://www.libertynet.org/nol/natl.html** and click on the **Community** button at the top of the page. Click on the **NetAction** button under *Community Networking*. Now, go to **http://www.moveon.org** (Move On). We're just beginning to see the potential of the Internet as an organizing tool.

■ What, if anything, was interesting about these sites? Is there anything that can be used for social work? If so, what and how?

Exercise

Go to the Detroit Community AIDS Library at **http://www.libraries.wayne.edu/dcal/aids.html.** Click on the <u>PubMed</u> link under <u>Searchable Databases</u>. This takes you to a free Medline search page, which is a wonderful resource for finding any health-related resource.

■ How useful might this resource be for you in your practice?

Exercise

Go to NetPsych.com at **http://netpsych.com/.** This site explores the new uses of the Internet to deliver psychological and health care services. NetPsych is the first site to focus exclusively on online resources. Click the <u>HUH?</u> Button.

■ What do you think of the sites you find linked here?

■ What are your impressions of online psychotherapy? Should the social work profession consider an amendment to the Code of Ethics to cover practice in such circumstances?

part

2

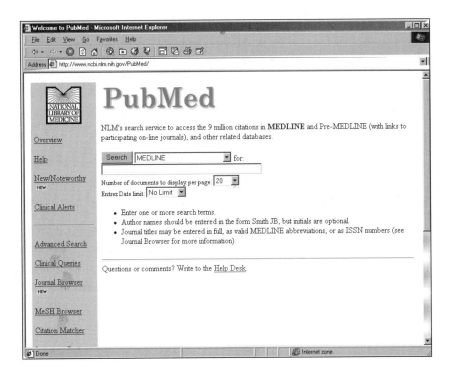

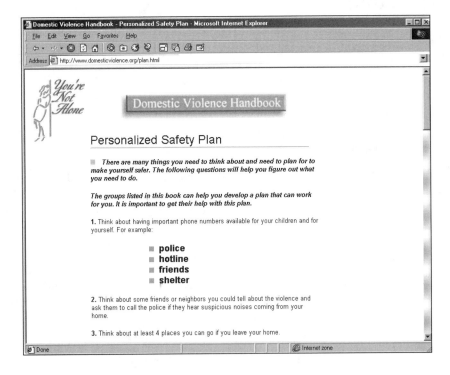

Exercise

Go to the Domestic Violence Handbook at **http://www.domesticviolence. org/**. This online resource is designed to assist women who are experiencing domestic abuse. Click on <u>Index</u> at the bottom of the page and follow the link to <u>Personalized Safety Plan</u>

▪ Would you be comfortable knowing that some victims of domestic violence have no other resources to help them? Why or why not?

List of URLs for Social Work

The Social Work Megasites

part
2

Association of Baccalaureate Social Work Program Directors

`http://www.rit.edu/~694www/bpd.htm`

This Web site, which serves as a home page for the BSW program directors, offers a variety of links to a wide range of social work Internet resources.

Columbia University Social Work Library

`http://www.columbia.edu/cu/libraries/indiv/socwk/`

Provides links to social work subject guides and Internet resources, social work related electronic journals on the Internet, and current social work monographs from Columbia University.

The Complete Social Worker Guide to Using the Internet in Social Work

`http://www.geocities.com/Heartland/4862/cswhome.html`

This online organization strives to create the most comprehensive knowledge base of social work professionals, educators, and students on the Web. They provide an impressive set of links to social work resources in a wide range of practice areas.

Computer Use in Social Services Network (CUSSN)

http://www.uta.edu/cussn/

CUSSNet began in 1985 as a group of FIDONET bulletin boards. Possibly the first social work presence on the Internet, no set of links would be complete without including reference to this site. The site provides links to resources related to computer use in human services, and serves as an important linkage for social workers on the Internet.

CTI: Social Work on the Web

http://www.soton.ac.uk/~chst/webconn.htm

This site is sponsored by the Computers in Teaching Initiative Centre for Human Services at the University of Southampton (UK). The site provides links in the areas of children and families, community work, social work databases, drugs, eldercare, equal opportunities, human rights, mental health, networks, psychosocial palliative care, social work organizations, social work practice, social work research, social work education, welfare benefits, and more.

Grassroots Social Work Resource Locator

http://www.andrews.edu/SOWK/grassroots.htm

Sponsored by the Social Work Department of Andrews University, this site offers keyword search capabilities and site reviews. The site also offers links to social work content areas, cross-curriculum issues, and other topics, such as social work education, professional organizations, spirituality and alternative therapies, social work technology, and social work journals and e-zines.

Nonprofit Resources Catalogue

http://www.clark.net/pub/pwalker/

This site, started by Phillip A. Walker as a personal project in 1994, has won numerous Web awards. It catalogues Internet sites that may benefit nonprofits and those interested in a wide variety of social work related issues. There is a heavy emphasis on meta-links to other catalogues in some subject areas.

The Phylis Lan Lin Program in Social Work Links and Lists

`http://socwork.uindy.edu/links/links.htm`

An impressive list of social work related links from the University of Indianapolis.

Social Work Access Network

`http://www.sc.edu/swan`

SWAN, sponsored by the University of South Carolina College of Social Work, offers one of the most complete listing of Internet resources available for social workers. SWAN organizes links in topical areas such as national organizations, global organizations, US governments, schools of social work, conferences and meeting, and topics by subject. SWAN also has listserv and newsgroup directories.

Social Work and Social Services Web Sites

`http://gwbweb.wustl.edu/websites.html`

Hosted by the George Warren Brown School of Social Work, this site offers a tremendous number of links in a wide range of social work practice areas.

part

2

The Social Work Café

`http://www.geocities.com/Heartland/4862/swcafe.html`

This site represents a wealth of resources in a variety of areas for social workers. Hosted as a free service of GeoCities.Com, the Social Work Café is a community of global Social Work professionals, educators, and students who believe in the cross-global exchange of information.

Social Work On-line

`http://www.socialworkonline.com/`

Created by Marvin P. Vernon, LCSW, this site is intended as a "one stop" site featuring the most valuable social work, social service, and mental health resources that the Internet has to offer. You will also find a chat room, featured articles, and some basic Internet advice.

World Wide Web Resources for Social Workers

http://www.nyu.edu/socialwork/wwwrsw/

W3RSW, produced by Gary Holden at NYU, is an amazing resource with what looks like hundreds of links to social work resources in a wide range of topics. This site was selected for the *Chronicle of Higher Education's Information Technology Resources* and for the *UniGuide Academic Guide to the Internet* (formerly the National Science Foundation funded *InterNIC Academic Guide to the Internet*).

Academic Sites

Columbia University (New York)

http://www.cc.columbia.edu/cu/ssw/

A particularly well-designed site, Columbia provides a variety of links to library, computing, and Internet resources for social work.

part
2

Colorado State University

http://www.colostate.edu/Depts/SocWork/

Colorado State provides a nice set of links to other Web resources

Florida International University

http://www.fiu.edu/~cupa/social-work.html

Provides a listing of WWW and Gopher sites for social work.

Grant MacEwan Community College (Alberta, Canada)

http://www.gmcc.ab.ca/nw/hcs/SWORK/

Great list of international social work resources, with a focus on Canada.

Jane Addams College of Social Work (Illinois)

http://www.uic.edu/jaddams/college/

This site includes information about Hull House Museum which commemorates the work of social welfare pioneer and peace advocate Jane

Addams, her innovative settlement house associates, and the neighborhood they served.

Memorial University of Newfoundland (Canada)

http://www.mun.ca/socwrk/

This site provides a number of links to links in the areas of social work, psychology, women's issues, justice and corrections, substance abuse, children's issues, men's issues, and social policy.

Michigan State University

http://www.ssc.msu.edu/~sw/

Provides a number of links to valuable Web resources, particularly in the areas of diversity, disabilities, and domestic violence.

New Mexico State University

http://www.nmsu.edu/~socwork/depthom.html

Provides information about the Family Preservation Institute and other social work related links.

North Carolina State University

http://www2.ncsu.edu/ncsu/chass/SocialWork/index.html

Offers links to social work resources in the areas of policy, practice methods, other points of interest for social work students.

Rochester Institute of Technology (New York)

http://www.isc.rit.edu/~694www/

This is a nicely designed site which offers resources related to social work and deafness and to social work and information technology.

Syracuse University (New York)

http://www.social.syr.edu/

Offers a comprehensive list of social work links in a wide variety of practice areas.

part

2

Temple University (Pennsylvania)

http://www.temple.edu/socialwork/

Offers some useful Internet resources for social workers.

University of Alabama

http://www.ua.edu/socwork/index.htm

Offers *Helping Hands: Social Work Resources on the Web*. Helping Hands was originally constructed by graduate students at the University of Alabama's School of Library and Information Studies. Helping Hands was designed to provide students enrolled at the University's School of Social Work with links to relevant World Wide Web resources that have been organized using fundamental principles of librarianship.

University of Bristol (UK)

http://www.bris.ac.uk/Depts/SPS/

The School for Policy Studies is the home of the Policy Press, and offers other social work links related to social policy in the United Kingdom.

University of Calgary (Alberta, Canada)

http://www.ucalgary.ca/SW/

Easy-to-use site offers resources which are useful to students, faculty and staff at the Faculty of Social Work and others in the social work field.

U. of California at Berkeley

http://hav54.socwel.berkeley.edu/

Berkeley offers a variety of links to social work resources on the Net.

University of Central Lancashire (UK)

http://www.uclan.ac.uk/facs/health/socwork/socihom1.htm

Provides access to lots of social work Web-sites including The Social Work Student, Britain's first online, student refereed journal and Professional Digest, a database of social work research.

University of Chicago (Illinois)

http://www.chas.uchicago.edu/ssa/

One of the most comprehensive information resources available to social workers, this site offers the Social Work Student Network (SWSN), a collaborative effort among student social workers throughout the world.

University of East Anglia, Norwich (UK)

http://www.uea.ac.uk/menu/acad_depts/swk/

Provides information about the Centre for Research on the Child and Family and the Family Support Network.

University of Kansas

http://www.socwel.ukans.edu/

Provides a bibliography for the strengths perspective in social work, social science resources, information from Office of Social Policy Analysis and the Kansas Kids Count home page.

University of Michigan

http://www.umich.edu/~socwk/ssw.html

Offers important resources for social work students and information about ongoing research at the University of Michigan.

University of Oxford (UK)

http://marx.apsoc.ox.ac.uk/

Provides information about current research at the University of Oxford, recent publications, and useful links.

University of Pennsylvania

http://www.ssw.upenn.edu

University of Pennsylvania is the home of PRAXIS, which provides resources for social and economic development. The site also provides information about current research at the University of Pennsylvania and international activities of the School of Social Work.

part 2

University of Plymouth (UK)

http://hs.plym.ac.uk/spsw.html

This site offers information about the Community Research Centre at the University of Plymouth, as well as links to social policy and social work related WWW pages.

University of South Carolina

http://www.sc.edu/cosw/index.html

The University of South Carolina is the home of the Social Work Access Network and sponsors an annual National Technology Conference for social work.

University of South Florida

http://www.cas.usf.edu/social_work/index.html

Provides a variety of resources for social work students which are useful for seasoned practitioners as well.

University of Southern California

http://www.usc.edu/dept/socialwork/home.htm

USC offers their Top Ten Internet resources in psychology and mental health, community organizing and welfare reform, social work research, industrial social work, family and children, health care, career development, government resources, foundations and grant making, nonprofits, and social work indexes.

University of Tennessee–Knoxville

http://www.csw.utk.edu/

Provides a social work discussion area, information about the Children's Mental Health Services Research Area, and links to other important resources.

University of Texas at Arlington

http://www2.uta.edu/ssw/

The home of CUSSNET (Computer Users in Human Services), UTA offers a variety of informational links for students and practitioners.

part
2

University of Texas at Austin

http://www.utexas.edu/depts/sswork/

Provides a listing of the activities of their Center for Social Work Research.

University of Utah Graduate School of Social Work

http://www.socwk.utah.edu

The home base of the author, the site provides information about ongoing research projects and related resources.

University of Washington

http://weber.u.washington.edu/~sswweb/index.html

In addition to the usual links, UW offers *Policy Watch*, a more-or-less weekly bulletin about issues and events in Olympia during the legislative session, focused primarily on social welfare, low-income, and related health concerns before the legislature.

University of Wisconsin–Madison

http://polyglot.lss.wisc.edu/socwork/intro.html

Offers information about The Institute for Research on Poverty, The LaFollette Institute of Public Policy, and the UW Homelessness Project.

University of York (UK)

http://www.york.ac.uk/depts/spsw/

This UK site offers a useful Social Policy Resource Guide.

Washington University: George Warren Brown School of Social Work (Missouri)

http://gwbweb.wustl.edu/

One of the most comprehensive sites in social work education, these pages offer information about research projects at GWB and a complete list of informational links in a variety of practice areas. The Social Work and Social Services Jobs Database is a valuable resource for all social workers.

part

2

Government Resources

Administration for Children and Families

http://www.acf.dhhs.gov

The Administration on Children, Youth and Families (ACYF) administers the major Federal programs that support: social services that promote the positive growth and development of children and youth and
their families; protective services and shelter for children and youth in
at-risk situations; child care for working families and families on public
assistance; and adoption for children with special needs.

Bureau of the Census

http://www.census.gov/

The Census Bureau Web site is designed to enable intuitive use of their
Internet offerings, so users need not to be familiar with the Census
Bureau's internal organizational structure to effectively locate and use
the resources the site has to offer.

Bureau of Labor Statistics

http://stats.bls.gov/

The Bureau of Labor Statistics (BLS) is the principal fact-finding agency
for the Federal Government in the broad field of labor economics and
statistics. The BLS is an independent national statistical agency that collects, processes, analyzes, and disseminates essential statistical data to
the American public, the U.S. Congress, other Federal agencies, State
and local governments, business, and labor. The BLS also serves as a
statistical resource to the Department of Labor.

Canadian Government Main Site

http://canada.gc.ca/

Government of Canada Primary Internet Site (Canada Site) is the Internet electronic access point through which Internet users around the
world can obtain information about Canada, its government and its services. Direct links are also provided from this site to government departments and agencies that have Internet facilities.

part
2

Catalog of Federal Domestic Assistance

http://aspe.os.dhhs.gov/cfda/

The Catalog of Federal Domestic Assistance Programs (CFDA) is a government-wide compendium of all 1,381 Federal programs, projects, services, and activities that provide assistance or benefits to the American public. These programs provide grants, loans, loan guarantees, services, information, scholarships, training, insurance, etc.

Centers for Disease Control

http://www.cdc.gov/

The Centers for Disease Control and Prevention (CDC), located in Atlanta, Georgia, USA, is an agency of the Department of Health and Human Services. Its mission is to promote health and quality of life by preventing and controlling disease, injury, and disability. The site provides health news, publications, software, data and statistics, and information about funding and programs.

part

2

Child Support Enforcement

http://www.acf.dhhs.gov/programs/CSE/

Child Support Enforcement helps States locate absent parents, establish paternity, and enforce legal orders for support.

Corporation for National Service

http://www.cns.gov/

Information about volunteer opportunities, including VISTA, Americorps, Senior Corps, Learn and Serve America, and National Service Scholarships.

Department of Health and Human Services (DHHS)

http://www.os.dhhs.gov

The Department of Health and Human Services is the United States government's principal agency for protecting the health of all Americans and providing essential human services, especially for those who are least able to help themselves. It is the largest grant-making agency in the federal government, providing some 60,000 grants per year. HHS'

Medicare program is the nation's largest health insuror, handling more than 800 million claims per year.

Empowerment Zones and Enterprise Communities Internet Home Page

http://www.ezec.gov/

The Empowerment Zone/Enterprise Communities Home Page is designed to promote the exchange of information about the Presidential Empowerment Initiative. Here you will find information about the purposes and organization of the Initiative and the Empowerment Zones, Enterprise Communities, and Champion Communities participating in the Initiative. In addition, the EZ/EC Home Page provides a toolbox of information to help communities develop and implement effective strategic plans for community and economic development.

Federal Emergency Management Agency

http://www.fema.gov/

The Federal Emergency Management Agency (FEMA) is an independent agency of the federal government, reporting to the President. Founded in 1979, FEMA's mission is to reduce loss of life and property and protect our nation's critical infrastructure from all types of hazards through a comprehensive, risk-based, emergency management program of mitigation, preparedness, response and recovery.

FedWorld Information Network Home Page

http://www.fedworld.gov

Access to thousands of U.S. Government Web sites, more than a ½ million U.S. government documents, databases, and other information products.

Government Information Sharing Project

http://govinfo.kerr.orst.edu/

The Government Information Sharing Project was initiated with funding from the U.S. Department of Education and is administered at Oregon State University Libraries. The original goal of the Project was to demonstrate improved access to electronic government information, especially for remote users (such as rural Oregon residents) and the general public. Beginning in 1995, the Project developed World Wide Web access to a variety of federal statistical information issued on CD-ROM and distributed through the Federal Depository Library Program. Through the Web, the audience of the site has quickly become a national and international one, including libraries, community developers, small and large businesses, researchers, students, journalists, agencies, and many more.

Government Printing Office

http://www.access.gpo.gov/

The Government Printing Office (GPO) prints, binds, and distributes the publications of the Congress as well as the executive departments and establishments of the Federal Government. Distribution is being accomplished on an increasing basis via various electronic media in accordance with Public Law 103–40, "The Government Printing Office Electronic Information Access Enhancement Act of 1993."

part

2

Health Care Financing Administration

http://www.hcfa.gov/

The Health Care Financing Administration (HCFA), the federal agency that administers the Medicare, Medicaid and Child Health Insurance Programs. HCFA provides health insurance for over 74 million Americans through Medicare, Medicaid and Child Health. The majority of these individuals receive their benefits through the Fee-for-Service delivery system, however, an increasing number are choosing managed care plans. In addition to providing health insurance, HCFA also regulates all laboratory testing (except research) in the U.S. through the Clinical Laboratory Improvement Amendments (CLIA) program.

healthfinder

http://www.healthfinder.org/

healthfinder™ is a gateway consumer health and human services information Web site from the United States government. healthfinder™ can lead you to selected online publications, clearinghouses, databases, Web sites, and support and self-help groups, as well as the government agencies and not-for-profit organizations that produce reliable information for the public. Launched in April 1997, healthfinder™served Internet users over 1.7 million times in its first year online.

Health Resources and Services Administration

http://www.hrsa.dhhs.gov

The Health Resources and Services Administration (HRSA) directs national health programs which improve the health of the Nation by assuring quality health care to underserved, vulnerable and special-need populations and by promoting appropriate health professions workforce capacity and practice, particularly in primary care and public health.

House of Representatives

http://www.house.gov

Contact your congressional representative the easy way.

Improving Services for Hispanics

http://phs.os.dhhs.gov/about/heo/hispanic.html

Hispanics are the fastest growing minority population in the U.S. and are predicted to be the largest minority group in the next 15 years. The adverse social conditions suffered by many Hispanics are severely challenging those institutions and service structures which struggle to provide and deliver quality services to Hispanic families and communities. HHS is mandated to work more closely with its partner institutions and organizations that serve the Hispanic community to better address their needs. As one of many efforts to meet this challenge, they have established the Hispanic Home Page to serve as a departmental Internet link for improving service delivery. The Hispanic Home Page features services provided by the Department that are of particular interest to the Hispanic community and organizations serving Hispanics.

Indian Health Service

http://www.tucson.ihs.gov/

The Indian Health Service (IHS), an agency within the Department of Health and Human Services, is responsible for providing federal health services to American Indians and Alaska Natives. The provision of health services to members of federally-recognized tribes grew out of the special government-to-government relationship between the federal government and Indian tribes.

Library of Congress

http://lcweb.loc.gov/

The Library of Congress mission is to make its resources available and useful to the Congress and the American people and to sustain and preserve a universal collection of knowledge and creativity for future generations. This World Wide Web site allows the Library of Congress to historical collections, their catalog, the text and images from major exhibitions, the THOMAS database of current and historical information on the U.S. Congress, a Learning Page for K–12 students and teachers, and much more.

Maternal and Child Health Bureau

http://www.os.dhhs.gov/hrsa/mchb

The Maternal and Child Health Bureau (MCHB) is charged with the primary responsibility for promoting and improving the health of our Nation's mothers and children. It predecessor, the Children's Bureau, was established in 1912. In 1935, Congress enacted Title V of the Social Security Act, which authorized the Maternal and Child Health Services Programs—providing a foundation and structure for assuring the health of mothers and children now for more than 60 years. Today, Title V is administered by the Maternal and Child Health Bureau as part of the Health Resources and Services Administration, Public Health Service, U.S. Department of Health and Human Services.

part

2

National Association of State Information Resource Executive's StateSearch

http://www.nasire.org/statesearch/

StateSearch is a service of the National Association of State Information Resource Executives and is designed to serve as a topical clearinghouse to state government information on the Internet.

National Cancer Institute

http://www.nci.nih.gov/

The National Cancer Institute (NCI) is a component of the National Institutes of Health (NIH), one of eight agencies that compose the Public Health Service (PHS) in the Department of Health and Human Services (DHHS). The NCI, established under the National Cancer Act of 1937, is the Federal Government's principal agency for cancer research and training. The National Cancer Act of 1971 broadened the scope and responsibilities of the NCI and created the National Cancer Program. Over the years, legislative amendments have maintained the NCI authorities and responsibilities and added new information dissemination mandates as well as a requirement to assess the incorporation of state-of-the-art cancer treatments into clinical practice.

National Clearinghouse for Alcohol and Drug Information

http://www.health.org

The National Clearinghouse for Alcohol and Drug Information, NCADI, is the world's largest repository of information on substance abuse prevention and policy. Information on drug and alcohol abuse, alcoholism prevention, overdoses, addiction, and treatment is available in thousands of documents, searchable databases, statistics, press releases, public domain graphics, and interactive forums.

National Criminal Justice Reference Service

http://www.ncjrs.org/

The National Criminal Justice Reference Service (NCJRS) is one of the most extensive sources of information on criminal and juvenile justice in the world, providing services to an international community of policymakers and professionals. NCJRS is a collection of clearinghouses supporting all bureaus of the U.S. Department of Justice, Office of Justice Programs: the National Institute of Justice, the Office of Juvenile Justice and Delinquency Prevention, the Bureau of Justice Statistics, the Bureau of Justice Assistance, the Office for Victims of Crime, and the OJP Program Offices. It also supports the Office of National Drug Control Policy.

National Institute of Alcohol Abuse and Alcoholism

http://www.niaaa.nih.gov/

In 1970, the United States Congress recognized alcohol abuse and alcoholism as major public health problems and created the National Institute on Alcohol Abuse and Alcoholism (NIAAA) to combat them. The

Web site provides information about reports and publications available from the Institute, as well as access to the ETOH database.

National Institute of Child Health and Human Development

http://www.nih.gov/nichd

The National Institute of Child Health and Human Development is part of the National Institutes of Health, U.S. Department of Health and Human Services. The NICHD conducts and supports laboratory, clinical and epidemiological research on the reproductive, neurobiologic, developmental, and behavioral processes that determine and maintain the health of children, adults, families and populations.

National Institute of Drug Abuse

http://www.nida.nih.gov

The National Institute on Drug Abuse (NIDA) supports over 85 percent of the world's research on the health aspects of drug abuse and addiction, ranging from the most fundamental and essential questions about drug abuse; the molecule to managed care, and from DNA to community outreach research. The NIDA Web page is an important part of NIDA's effort to ensure the rapid and effective transfer of scientific data to policy makers, drug abuse practitioners, other health care practitioners and the general public.

part

2

National Institutes of Health

http://www.nih.gov/

The NIH mission is to uncover new knowledge that will lead to better health for everyone. NIH works toward that mission by: conducting research in its own laboratories; supporting the research of non-Federal scientists in universities, medical schools, hospitals, and research institutions throughout the country and abroad; helping in the training of research investigators; and fostering communication of biomedical information.

National Institute of Mental Health

http://www.nimh.nih.gov/

NIMH is the foremost mental health research organization in the world, with a mission of improving the treatment, diagnosis, and prevention of mental disorders such as schizophrenia and depressive illnesses, and other conditions that affect millions of Americans, including children and adolescents. The Web site provides information about mental health disorders, news and events, grants and contracts, and NIMH-sponsored research activities.

National Library of Medicine

http://www.nlm.nih.gov/

The NLM site provides individuals free access to MEDLINE for free. The visible human project and other offerings make this a "must browse" site.

Office of Population Affairs

http://phs.os.dhhs.gov/progorg/opa/

The Office of Population Affairs provides resources and policy advice on population, family planning, reproductive health, and adolescent pregnancy issues. OPA also administers two grant programs, the national Family Planning Program and the Adolescent Family Life Program.

Rural Housing Service

http://www.rurdev.usda.gov/agency/rhs/rhs.html

The USDA Rural Housing Service has various programs available to aid in the development of rural America. Rural Housing programs are divided into three categories: Community Facilities (CF), Single Family Housing (SFH), and Multi-Family Housing (MFH). These programs were formerly operated by the Rural Development Administration and the Farmers Home Administration.

Senate Home Page

http://www.senate.gov/

Contact your Senators the easy way.

Social Security Administration

http://www.ssa.gov

part
2

This site provides a wealth of information about the Social Security Administration, enabling users to better the negotiate the maze of services available.

Substance Abuse and Mental Health Services Administration

http://www.samhsa.gov/

SAMHSA's mission is to assure that quality substance abuse and mental health services are available to the people who need them and to ensure that prevention and treatment knowledge is used more effectively in the general health care system.

Thomas—U.S. Congress on the Internet

http://thomas.loc.gov/

Current US Federal Legislative Information, including bills, laws, Congressional Record, reports, and links to further information.

Veterans Affairs

http://www.va.gov/

The Department of Veterans Affairs (VA) Web site provides information on VA programs, veterans benefits, VA facilities worldwide, and VA medical automation software. The site serves several major constituencies including the veteran and his/her dependents, Veterans Service Organizations, the military, the general public, and VA employees around the world. Documents on the site are linked from their table of contents and searchable by keyword.

White House

http://www.whitehouse.gov

The executive branch of the United States government. Even Socks has a page.

YouthInfo

http://youth.os.dhhs.gov/

YouthInfo is a Web site developed by the U.S. Department of Health and Human Services (HHS) to provide individuals with the latest information

part

2

about America's adolescents. YouthInfo currently includes the following: a statistical profile of America's teenagers; the latest reports and publications about adolescents; information for parents of teens; speeches by federal officials on youth topics; links to youth-related Web sites at HHS, other federal agencies and private foundations and research organizations.

Professional Association Sites

Alliance for Psychosocial Nursing

http://www.psychnurse.org/

The APN is the primary organization for psychiatric and mental health nurses worldwide. The site serves as a resource and lobbying force for nurses and their patients and contains information about memberships and meetings, a job bank, online journal, and discussion areas.

American Association of Community Psychiatrists

http://www3.pitt.edu/~kthomp

The AACP seeks to promote and maintain excellence in the care of patients through the organization of psychiatrists practicing community mental health on state, regional and national levels.

American Association for Marriage and Family Therapy

http://www.aamft.org/

The American Association for Marriage and Family Therapy (AAMFT) is the professional association for the field of marriage and family therapy. We represent the professional interests of more than 23,000 marriage and family therapists throughout the United States, Canada and abroad.

American Association of Pastoral Counselors

http://www.metanoia.org/aapc/

Pastoral Counseling is a mental health discipline that integrates psychotherapy and spirituality. Pastoral Counselors are mental health professionals who have received specialized graduate training in both religion and the behavioral sciences, and practice the integrated discipline of pastoral counseling. The American Association of Pastoral Counselors (AAPC) represents and sets professional standards for over 3,200 Pastoral Counselors and more than 100 pastoral counseling centers in the United States.

American Association of Health Plans

http://www.aahp.org

The American Association of Health Plans (AAHP), located in Washington, DC, represents more than 1,000 HMOs, PPOs and other network-based plans. AAHP's member companies are dedicated to a philosophy of health care that puts the patient-first; together they care for close to 140 million Americans nationwide.

American Association of State Social Work Boards

http://www.aasswb.org/

The American Association of State Social Work Boards (AASSWB) is the association of state bodies that regulate social work. Incorporated in 1979 as an organization devoted to consumer protection, AASSWB membership now includes all 50 states, the District of Columbia, and the Virgin Islands.

part
2

American Counseling Association

http://www.counseling.org

The American Counseling Association is a not-for-profit, professional and educational organization that is dedicated to the growth and enhancement of the counseling profession.

American Medical Association

http://www.ama-assn.org

Since its founding in 1847 by a group of physicians concerned about advancing the quality of medical education, science, and practice, the American Medical Association's core purpose has been to promote the art and science of medicine and the betterment of public health.

American Mental Health Counselors Association

http://www.amhca.org

The mission of the American Mental Health Counselors Association is to enhance the profession of mental health counseling through licensing, advocacy, education, and professional development. Their vision is to be the national organization representing licensed mental health counselors, and state chapters, with consistent standards of education, training, licensing, practice, advocacy, and ethics.

American Psychiatric Association

http://www.psych.org/

The American Psychiatric Association is a medical specialty society recognized world-wide. Its 40,500 U.S. and international physicians specialize in the diagnosis and treatment of mental and emotional illnesses and substance use disorders.

American Public Health Association

http://www.apha.org/

The American Public Health Association (APHA) is the oldest and largest organization of public health professionals in the world, representing more than 50,000 members from over 50 occupations of public health.

Association for the Advancement of Social Work with Groups

http://dominic.barry.edu/~kelly/aaswg/aaswg.html

AASWG is an international professional organization that provides advocacy and action in support of social work group work practice, education, research, and publication.

Association of Baccalaureate Program Directors

http://www.rit.edu/~694www/bpd.htm

This professional association represents directors of baccalaureate social work programs accredited through the Council on Social Work Education.

part

2

Association for Behavior Analysis

http://www.wmich.edu/aba/

The Association for Behavior Analysis is dedicated to promoting the experimental, theoretical, and applied analysis of behavior. It encompasses contemporary scientific and social issues, theoretical advances, and the dissemination of professional and public information.

Association for Oncology Social Work

http://www.biostat.wisc.edu/aosw/aoswhello.html

A nonprofit, international organization dedicated to the enhancement of psychosocial services to people with cancer and their families.

Australian Association of Social Work

http://www.aasw.asn.au/

The objectives of the Australian Association of Social Workers Ltd are to promote the profession of social work, to provide an organisation through which social workers can develop a professional identity, to establish, monitor and improve practice standards, to contribute to the development of social work knowledge, to advocate on behalf of clients, and to actively support social structures and policies pursuant to the promotion of social justice.

part

2

British Association of Social Workers

http://www.basw.demon.co.uk/

BASW is the largest organization of professional social workers in the United Kingdom. They speak on all issues which affect the professional standing of social work. Members come from a wide range of agencies in the Local Authority, Voluntary, Independent and Private sectors throughout the United Kingdom. BASW campaigns for improvements to legislation, for social justice and the quality of social work services and good practice.

Clinical Social Work Federation

http://www.webcom.com/nfscsw/

The Clinical Social Work Federation is a confederation of 31 state societies for clinical social work. Their state societies are formed as voluntary associations for the purpose of promoting the highest standards of professional education and clinical practice. Each society is active with legislative advocacy and lobbying efforts for adequate and appropriate mental health services and coverage at their state and national levels of government.

Computer Use in Social Services Network

http://www.uta.edu/cussn/

The Computer Use in Social Services Network (CUSSN) is an informal association of professionals interested in exchanging information and experiences on using computers in the human services. It has been in existence since 1981.

Council on Social Work Education

http://www.cswe.org

CSWE is a national association that preserves and enhances the quality of social work education for practice that promotes the goals of individual and community well-being and social justice. CSWE pursues this mission through setting and maintaining policy and program standards, accrediting bachelor's and master's degree programs in social work, promoting research and faculty development, and advocating for social work education.

Institute for Mental Health Initiatives

http://www.imhi.org/

Institute for Mental Health Initiatives (IMHI), a nonprofit organization of mental health professionals, promotes emotional well-being in children, families, and their communities. It makes mental health research accessible to the media and the general public. IMHI builds bridges between clinicians and researchers in the field of mental health, the general public, and the members of the media.

International Association of Group Psychotherapy

http://www.psych.mcgill.ca/labs/iagp/

The purpose of the IAGP is to serve the development of group psychotherapy, as a field of practice, training, and scientific study, by means of international conferences, publications, and other forms of communication. The assumption is that there is mutual respect between representatives of differing theories and practices concerned with the use and study of group resources in psychotherapy and in dealing eith other human problems.

International Federation of Social Workers

http://www.ifsw.org/

The International Federation of Social Workers is a successor to the International Permanent Secretariat of Social Workers, which was founded in Paris in 1928 and was active until the outbreak of World War II. It was not until 1950, at the time of the International Conference of Social Work in Paris, that the decision was made to create the International Federation of Social Workers, an international organization of professional social workers.

Irish Association of Social Workers

http://ireland.iol.ie/~iasw/

The Irish Association of Social Workers (IASW) was founded in 1971. It is the national organization of professional social workers in the Republic of Ireland.

Mental Health in Corrections Consortium

http://www.mhcca.org/

MHCC is dedicated to being a leading voice for mental health providers within the criminal justice system, primarily corrections, and providing the highest quality of training related to mental health issues within criminal justice.

National Association of Social Workers (NASW)

http://www.socialworkers.org/

NASW is the largest association of professional social workers in the United States. With 155,000 members in 55 chapters, NASW promotes, develops and protects the practice of social work and social workers. NASW also seeks to enhance the well-being of individuals, families, and communities through its work and through its advocacy.

part

2

National Association of State Mental Health Program Directors

http://www.nasmhpd.org/

The National Association of State Mental Health Program Directors (NASMHPD) organizes to reflect and advocate for the collective interests of State Mental Health Authorities and their directors at the national level. NASMHPD analyzes trends in the delivery and financing of mental health services and builds and disseminates knowledge and experience reflecting the integration of public mental health programming in evolving healthcare environments.

National Council for Community Behavioral Healthcare

http://www.nccbh.org/

The National Council for Community Behavioral Healthcare was founded in 1970 to implement a vision and set of beliefs through membership, advocacy and education. Through their work In the public interest, they advocate before the White House, Congress, and federal agencies to advance the interests of our members and the consumers that they serve.

National Coalition of Hispanic Health and Human Services Organizations

http://www.cossmho.org/

COSSMHO is the sole organization focusing on the health, mental health, and human services needs of the diverse Hispanic communities. COSSMHO's membership consists of thousands of front-line health and human services providers and organizations serving Hispanic communities. The organization was founded in Los Angeles in 1973 as the Coalition of Spanish-Speaking Mental Health Organizations to represent and advocate for the mental health needs of Mexican American, Puerto Rican, Cuban American, Central American, and South American communities in the United States.

National Institute for Social Work

http://www.nisw.org.uk/

The National Institute for Social Work is the only independent national organization in the United Kingdom specializing exclusively in the personal social services. Founded over 30 years ago, the Institute is at the forefront of social work and social care, actively raising standards and promoting good practice in the public, independent, and voluntary sectors.

Society for Social Work Leadership in Health Care

http://www.sswlhc.org/

The Society for Social Work Leadership in Health Care is an association, 1,500 members strong, dedicated to promoting the universal availability, accessibility, coordination, and effectiveness of health care that addresses the psychosocial components of health and illness.

World Federation of Mental Health

http://www.wfmh.com

The World Federation for Mental Health is an international nonprofit advocacy organization founded in 1948 to advance, among all peoples and nations, the prevention of mental and emotional disorders, the proper treatment and care of those with such disorders, and the promotion of mental health. The Federation achieves its goals through public education programs such as World Mental Health Day, research through collaborating centers at major universities, consultation to the United Nations and its specialized agencies, and a regional structure for organizing project work at the community level.

part

2

Electronic Journals and Newsletters

The Advocate's Forum

http://www.ssa.uchicago.edu/advocates_forum.html

A social work journal managed entirely by University of Chicago students with support from the Office of External Affairs. Inside you will find substantive articles reflecting the diversity of interests, ideas, and concerns of social work students and graduates.

Age and Aging

http://www.oup.co.uk/jnls/list/ageing/

An international journal publishing refereed original articles and commissioned reviews on geriatric medicine and gerontology. Its range includes research on aging and clinical, epidemiological, and psychological aspects of later life.

AIDS Book Review Journal

http://www.library.ucsb.edu/journals/aids/

An electronic journal reviewing books, videos, journal titles, and other materials covering AIDS, safer sex, sexually transmitted diseases, and other related materials, published irregularly by the University of Illinois at Chicago Library.

Alcohol Alerts

http://silk.nih.gov/silk/niaaa1/publication/
alalerts.htm

A quarterly bulletin of the National Institute on Alcohol Abuse and Alcoholism that disseminates important research findings on a single aspect of alcohol abuse and alcoholism.

American Journal on Addictions

http://www.appi.org/ajatoc61.html

Contents of issues and abstracts of articles from *AJA,* an authoritative source of new information on drug abuse and the addictions.

American Medical Association Publishing

http://www.ama-assn.org/scipub.htm

Web editions of the AMA's Scientific Publications and American Medical News and links to condition-specific Web sites.

APA Addictions Newsletter

http://www.kumc.edu/addictions_newsletter/

An online publication of The American Psychological Association, Division 50.

APA Journals

http://www.apa.org/journals/

A listing of all journals published by the American Psychological Association.

American Psychiatric Press

`http://www.appi.org/`

An overview of the publications of the American Psychiatric Press, Inc.

Behavior Therapy

`http://server.psyc.vt.edu/aabt/bt/home`

Tables of contents and abstracts for a journal of the Association for Advancement of Behavior Therapy.

Canadian Journal of Behavioural Science

`http://www.cpa.ca/ac-main.html`

Abstracts and full-text versions of articles.

Child and Adolescent Psychiatry

`http://www.priory.co.uk/psychild.htm`

Online journal featuring articles relevant to the treatment of children and adolescents.

Child Maltreatment: Journal of the American Professional Society on the Abuse of Children

`http://157.142.136.54/cm/cmhome.htm`

Child Maltreatment is the main APSAC vehicle for publishing longer and more in-depth analyses of theoretical, practice, and policy issues. In addition, CM is an outlet for high-quality original empirical research and reviews of the research literature.

Child Welfare Review

`http://www.childwelfare.com/kids/news.htm`

An electronic journal for coverage of issues related to the well-being of children. It contains both links to articles related to child welfare and original articles.

part

2

The Chronicle of Philanthropy

http://philanthropy.com/

The Chronicle of Philanthropy is an important news source for charity leaders, fund raisers, grant makers, and other people involved in the philanthropic enterprise.

Cognitive and Behavioral Practice

http://server.psyc.vt.edu/aabt/cbp/home

Another journal of the Association for Advancement of Behavior Therapy.

Computers in Human Services

http://www.uta.edu/cussn/chs.html

Computers in Human Services is a journal dedicated to providing information about the use of computer-based information technologies in the human services. It is designed for practitioners as well as instructors.

Current Research in Social Psychology

http://www.uiowa.edu/~grpproc/crisp/crisp.html

A peer reviewed, electronic journal covering all aspects of social psychology sponsored by the Center for the Study of Group Processes at the University of Iowa.

Electronic Journals and Periodicals in Psychology and Related Fields

http://psych.hanover.edu/Krantz/journal.html

A regularly updated listing of psychology-relevant journals.

The Future of Children

http://www.futureofchildren.org/

Produced by The Center for the Future of Children, The David and Lucile Packard Foundation, The Future of Children is published three times a year and (mostly) reproduced on this site. Links to previous editions are available.

part
2

Harvard Mental Health Letter

http://www.countway.med.harvard.edu/publications/Heal
th_Publications/mntlns.html

Selected articles from the publication.

Hunger Notes

http://www.brown.edu/Departments/World_Hunger_Program
/hungerweb/HN/HNHomePg.html

Hunger Notes is an online journal which is sponsored by the World
Hunger Education Service.

Journal of Applied Behavior Analysis

http://www.envmed.rochester.edu/wwwrap/behavior/jaba/

Abstracts and tables of contents.

Journal of Children and Poverty

http://www.carfax.co.uk/jcp-ad.htm

The Journal of Children and Poverty is a publication of the Institute for
Children and Poverty, the research and training division of Homes for
the Homeless. It offers a forum for the presentation of research and policy initiatives in the areas of education, social services, public policy, and
welfare reform as they affect children, youth, and families in poverty.

Journal of Cognitive Rehabilitation

http://www.inetdirect.net/nsp/

A specialized online magazine containing general interest articles, personal
experience articles, research reports and computerized therapy exercises
related to brain injury, head injury, and strokes.

Journal of Mind and Behavior

http://kramer.ume.maine.edu/~jmb/

Journal related to cross-causal understanding of cognition and behavior.
Contents and abstracts of articles in past issues.

part

2

The Journal of Online Behavior (JOB)

http://www.behavior.net/JOB/

JOB is concerned with the empirical study of human behavior in the online environment, and with the impact of evolving communication and information technology upon individuals, groups, organizations, and society. It is a peer-reviewed, behavioral science/social science journal, with editorial board members from several countries and disciplinary affiliations. The journal is published electronically on the World Wide Web, and in printed form. Each article published on the Web is accompanied by an interactive discussion space, a pointer to which will accompany the article site. Significant comments from discussions may accompany the paper publication.

Journal of Poverty

http://128.146.40.65/jpov/

The Journal of Poverty: Innovations on Social, Political and Economic Inequalities is the first refereed journal designed to provide a focused outlet for discourse on poverty and inequality.

Journal of Social Work Practice

http://www.carfax.co.uk/jsw-ad.htm

Journal devoted to social work practice from a psychodynamic perspective. Contents and abstracts of articles in past issues.

Links to Psychological Journals (by Armin Gunther)

http://www.psychwww.com/resource/journals.htm

An index of more than 1,500 links to psychology and social science journals online, this Web site covers English, French, and Dutch language journals, and provides general journal information, tables of contents, abstracts, or full text articles.

Lippincott's Nursing Center

http://www.nursingcenter.com/

The *American Journal of Nursing* was the first U.S. nursing publication to make a home on the World Wide Web. It has recently launched Lippincott's NursingCenter, which features full-text continuing education articles as well as tables of contents from the current *AJN*, summaries of articles, and links to sites for other nursing journals.

The New Social Worker

http://www.socialworker.com/

The New Social Worker is the only national magazine devoted to social work students and recent graduates. This Web site presents the online version of the magazine, and presents links to employment resources.

NIH Record

http://www.nih.gov/news/NIH-Record/archives.htm

The NIH Record is the biweekly newsletter for employees of the National Institutes of Health.

Philanthropy News Digest

http://fdncenter.org/phil/philmain.html

The Foundation Center publishes electronically its Philanthropy News Digest every week, highlighting philanthropy-related news from other print and electronic periodicals nationwide.

Psychiatric Times

http://www.mhsource.com/psychiatrictimes.html

Full text of news and clinical articles for psychiatrists, allied mental health professionals and primary care physicians who treat mental disorders.

Psychiatry on Line

http://www.priory.co.uk/psycont.htm

Current contents and more from the *International Journal of Psychiatry*.

Psychotherapy Finances and Managed Care Strategies

http://199.190.86.8/

News related to financing for psychotherapy and managed care.

part
2

Prevention Pipeline

http://www.health.org/pubs/prevpipe/

On-line publication of the National Clearinghouse for Alcohol and Drug Information.

PSYCHE

http://psyche.cs.monash.edu.au/

A refereed electronic journal dedicated to supporting the interdisciplinary exploration of the nature of consciousness and its relation to the brain.

Psychological Science Agenda

http://www.apa.org/psa/

The newsletter of the American Psychological Association Science Directorate.

part
2

Psycoloquy

http://www.princeton.edu/~harnad/psyc.html

A refereed international, interdisciplinary electronic journal sponsored by the American Psychological Association (APA), publishing target articles and peer commentary in all areas of psychology as well as cognitive science, neuroscience, behavioral biology, artificial intelligence, robotics/vision, linguistics and philosophy.

Qualitative Report

http://www.nova.edu/ssss/QR/

An online journal dedicated to qualitative research and critical inquiry.

Social Research Update

http://www.soc.surrey.ac.uk/sru/

A quarterly publication by the Department of Sociology, University of Surrey, England. Each issue cover s one topic in sufficient depth to indicate the main directions of recent developments and provide a bibliography for further reading.

Social Service Review

http://www.journals.uchicago.edu/SSR/

Contents and author notes from one of the premier journals in social work.

Sociological Research Online

http://www.soc.surrey.ac.uk/socresonline/

Online journal which publishes peer reviewed articles applying sociological analysis to a wide range of topics.

Standards: An International Journal of Multicultural Studies

http://stripe.Colorado.EDU/~standard/

An online publication featuring art, fiction, and scholarly essays relating to multicultural studies.

part

2

The Journal

http://www.arf.org/Intropage.html

Selected articles from print publication which provides news of interest to addictions professionals and those in related fields.

Social Work Areas of Practice Sites

ADMINISTRATION

Action Without Borders

http://www.idealist.org/

Organization with an aim to create a global network of community-based centers that will link, serve, and strengthen individuals and organizations working to build a better world.

A School's Guide to Getting On-Line

http://www.education-world.com/columns/past/
article-05a.shtml

```
http://www.education-world.com/columns/past/
article-05b.shtml
```

```
http://www.education-world.com/columns/past/
article-05c.shtml
```

```
http://www.education-world.com/columns/past/
article-05d.shtml
```

While prepared for schools, "A School's Guide to Getting On-Line" contains good information for any organization.

Aspen Institute

```
http://www.aspeninst.org
```

This site offers information on the activities and programs of the Aspen Institute in the US and in Germany, France, Italy and Japan. The Aspen institute is dedicated to the development of leadership in the nonprofit sector.

Best Practices Toolkit

```
http://www.benton.org/Practice/Toolkit/
```

This is a list of Internet and other resources aimed at helping nonprofits make better use of information and communications technologies in their work.

Charity and Community Service

```
http://www.einet.net/galaxy/Community/Charity-and-
Community-Service.html
```

EINet Galaxy hosts an array of pointers to information on the Internet including nonprofits in their Community section.

Council on Foundations

```
http://www.cof.org/
```

Features information on the Council, which is dedicated to assisting grantmakers become more effective funders and to supporting the growth of organized philanthropy.

Foundation Center

http://fdncenter.org/

A nonprofit information clearinghouse, providing information on foundations and corporate giving. The Center's site includes information on the Center, its libraries, seminars and publications. The site also features grantmaker information (including links to grantmaker Web sites), a searchable database of philanthropy-related articles, and a section on the fundraising process, including a proposal writing short course.

Free Management Library

http://www.mapnp.org/library/index.html

The Free Management Library (formerly the Nonprofit Managers' Library) facilitates sharing of free, online, and how-to management resources among nonprofits—including fundraising and grantwriting, marketing and public relations, using the Internet, and evaluation. The Management Assistance Program (MAP) for Nonprofits in St. Paul, Minnesota administers the library.

part

2

GuideStar

http://www.guidestar.org/

Information on the programs and finances of more than 600,000 American nonprofits organizations, with up-to-date news stories and features on philanthropy, and a forum for donors and volunteers.

Impact Online

http://www.impactonline.org/

A new organization that encourages community involvement by offering information on the Web about nonprofits with additional components for fundraising and volunteering.

Independent Sector

http://www.indepsec.org

Presents the various aspects of Independent Sector, a national coalition of voluntary organizations, foundations, and corporate giving programs, including information on Independent Sector's advocacy, research, and leadership programs.

Indiana University–Purdue University Indianapolis Library

http://www-lib.iupui.edu/subjectareas/philan.html

Pointers to a variety of resources from this library.

Information for Nonprofits

http://www.eskimo.com/~pbarber/

Home of the FAQ for soc.org.nonprofit and a number of other resources. The extensive FAQ answers many of the common questions about non-profit, from starting them to raising funds to using the Internet.

Internet Nonprofit Center

http://www.nonprofits.org

The site features the Nonprofit Locater, offering access to the IRS' Business Master File, which provides information on each charity in the Business Master File, including assets and revenues. The Center's site also offers a library of publications on nonprofits, a feature on the Top 40 Charities, and information on evaluating nonprofits and standards in philanthropy.

Introducing New Technology Successfully into an Agency

http://www.coyotecom.com/database/techbuy.html

Introducing computers to your agency, or upgrading software or hard-ware your agency uses, will change the way you access and manage in-formation—for the better, you hope. But without realistic expectations and a thoughtful strategy, a new system can create as many problems as it is supposed to solve. This tip sheet can help.

The Management Center

http://www.tmcenter.org

Helps nonprofit organizations manage better by providing consulting services in Northern California, conducting workshops and programs for professionals and board member, and producing a nonprofit job listing and an annual compensation survey.

National Center For Nonprofit Boards

`http://www.ncnb.org`

provides information on NCNB's activities, including its training, education, and consulting services for nonprofit Boards, as well as NCNB's National Leadership Forum. The site also features a catalog of materials on nonprofit governance published by the NCNB, and also includes a Board Information Center which provides answers and information on nonprofit governance.

National Opportunity NOCs

`http://www.opportunitynocs.org/`

A resource for nonprofit jobs and employment opportunities. Job seekers can conduct free searches through our large database of available nonprofit jobs online, while nonprofit organizations can post help wanted classified ads for job openings online. The site also features a career center, nonprofit library and additional nonprofit employment resources.

NGOnet—Central and Eastern Europe

`http://www.ngonet.org/`

NGONet has been created to provide information to, for and about nongovernmental organizations (NGOs) active in Central and Eastern Europe.

Nonprofit Cyber-Accountability

`http://www.bway.net/~hbograd/cyb-acc.html`

Offers the Cyber-Accountability listserv, an ongoing discussion on the nonprofit world and the use of information technology. The site also provides information on the National Accountability Research Project at the Nonprofit Coordinating Committee of New York, as well as links to other sites which contain information on nonprofits.

The Non-Profit Internet Handbook

`http://www.socialworker.com/nonprofit/npinter.htm`

The Non-Profit Internet Handbook is for nonprofit organizations that want to get the most out of the Internet. It is a valuable resource for executive staff, board members, those who donate funds, and those who contribute time to nonprofit organizations.

part

2

Paradigms

http://www.libertynet.org/rhd/Paradigms/

A virtual posting board for the nonprofit community providing an on-line forum to nonprofit projects, an exchange of innovations and revolutionary project strategies, and a directory of project models.

Philanthropy Journal Online

http://www.philanthropy-journal.org/

The Web site has extensive resources with alerts and links to many nonprofit sites, including a Meta-Index comprehensive text list of resources on the Internet of interest to nonprofits.

PRAXIS

http://www.ssw.upenn.edu/~restes/praxis.html

Resources for social and economic development; pointers to many resources created by Dr. Richard J. Estes at the University of Pennsylvania.

Urban Institute

http://www.urban.org/

Provides information on the activities of the Institute and its research and policy centers, and programs. The site also presents information on the Center on Nonprofits and the National Center on Charitable Statistics.

AGING

Administration on Aging

http://www.aoa.dhhs.gov/

Information about the Administration on Aging and its programs for the elderly, information about resources for practitioners who serve the aged, statistical information on the aging, and information for consumers (older persons and their families) including how to obtain services for senior citizens and electronic booklets on aging related issues. It also includes a link to AoA's National Aging Information Center and extensive links to other aging related Web resources.

part

2

Alzheimer's Association

`http://www.alz.org/`

The home page of the Alzheimer's association in the United States. Contains information about chapters, caregiver resources, medical information, public policy, and links to other resources.

Alzheimer's Disease Resource Page

`http://www.ohioalzcenter.org/`

Hosted by Case Western Reserve University, this page provides information on Alzheimer's Disease, for caregivers, practitioners, researchers, and the general public.

The ALZHEIMER Page

`http://www.biostat.wustl.edu/alzheimer`

A service of the Washington University (St. Louis) Alzheimer's Disease Research Center, this page provides links to just about everything you'd want to know about Alzheimer's disease, and in letters so big that you won't need your glasses.

part

2

ANSWERS

`http://www.service.com/answers/`

ANSWERS is a magazine for adult children of aging parents and is written for anyone facing the questions, issues, and concerns from having an aging parent. The site provides tables of contents for recent issues and full text of selected articles.

APA Division 20

`http://www.iog.wayne.edu/APADIV20/apadiv20.htm`

The home page of Division 20 of the American Psychological Association (Adult Development and Aging). This site provides information about the mission of Division 20, research and employment opportunities, pre- and post-doctoral programs of study in adult development and aging, instructional resources for teachers of adult development and aging, directory of members, contact information for specific laboratories/centers and institutes, and a Resource Guide for Clinicians.

Association for Gerontology Education in Social Work: AGE-SW

http://www.cs.umd.edu/users/connie/

Provides information about the organization, gerontology-related resources, and highlights from *AGEnda,* the AGE-SW newsletter.

DeathNET

http://www.IslandNet.com:80/~deathnet

Specializes in information concerning: euthanasia, suicide, assisted suicide, living wills, patient's rights, terminal illnesses such as ALS, cancer, multiple sclerosis, AIDS, heart disease, among others; hospice care, palliative care; "right to die" legislation; "self-deliverance"; and other aspects of death and dying. Also houses archives of Dr. Jack Kevorkian, Derek Humphry, right to die, and dying with dignity themes.

Family Caregiver Alliance

http://www.caregiver.org/

Information about the Family Caregiver Alliance, resource centers in California, caregiver tips, statistics and research, public policy, information about educational programs and conferences, publications, and more.

Geropsychology Central

http://www.premier.net/~gero/geropsyc.html

Devoted to the study of the neurological, psychological, sociological aspects of the aging process. Designed for the gerontological professional, seniors, and caregivers, features and links are topically organized for quick reference.

Grand Times

http://www.grandtimes.com/mags/

An online magazine for active retirees.

Michigan Alzheimer's Disease Research Center

http://www.med.umich.edu/madrc/MADRC.html

Provides information about the activities of the MADRC, their research projects, publications, programs for patients and families, and links to other Alzheimer's centers and programs and resources.

Multidisciplinary Education in Geriatrics and Aging

```
http://cpmcnet.columbia.edu/dept/dental/
Dental_Educational_Software/Gerontology_and_
Geriatric_Dentistry/introduction.html
```

Web-based course in aging for clinicians. Excellent resource.

National Council on Aging

```
http://www.ncoa.org/
```

An association of more than 7,500 members who work with, for, and on behalf of older persons. The organization is devoted "to promoting the dignity, self-determination, well-being, and contributions of older persons and to enhancing the field of aging through leadership and service, education, and advocacy . . ."

part

2

Senior Net

```
http://www.seniornet.org/
```

SeniorNet is a national nonprofit organization whose mission is to build a community of computer-using senior citizens. The site contains all kinds of information for and about seniors, instructional information on computing, and message boards and chat to enable seniors to contact each other.

Senior Sites

```
http://www.seniorsites.com/
```

This site may be the most comprehensive Web source of nonprofit housing and services for seniors. With over 5000 listed communities, Senior Sites is a valuable resource for seniors and their families interested in exploring the nonprofit housing option.

The University of Georgia Gerontology Center

```
http://www.geron.uga.edu/
```

Highlights the activities of the center, and provides links to other resources, including aging-related grants information.

CHILDREN, ADOLESCENTS, AND FAMILIES

Adolescent Directory On-Line

http://education.indiana.edu/cas/adol/

Adolescence Directory On-Line (ADOL) is an electronic guide to information on adolescent issues. It is a service of the Center for Adolescent Studies at Indiana University. Educators, counselors, parents, researchers, health practitioners, and teens can use ADOL to find Web resources on conflict and violence, mental health issues, health issues, counselor resources, and even help with homework.

American Academy of Child and Adolescent Psychiatry

http://www.aacap.org/

AACAP is a dynamic organization, giving direction to and responding quickly to new developments in health care, and addressing the needs of children, adolescents and families. Resources are provided to educate parents and families about psychiatric disorders affecting children and adolescents.

Casa de los Niños

http://www.azstarnet.com/~casa/

The mission of Casa de los Niños is the prevention, intervention, and treatment of child abuse and neglect by providing: residential shelter care for children who are abused, neglected, or homeless; supportive counseling to families; and community education. The Web site features information about the organization, child abuse statistics, information for parents, and links to related resources.

Center for Adolescent Studies

http://education.indiana.edu/cas/

The Center for Adolescent Studies at Indiana University focuses on meeting the social and emotional growth and development needs of adolescents through providing support to adults working with youth, investigating current social issues and providing tools for teens to learn and practice new, healthy behaviors. Links are provided to Center programs, which include research projects, support for teachers, and a computer-based decision aide to help schools select the drug prevention program most likely to meet their needs.

Child Welfare

http://www.childwelfare.com/

Provides a gateway to information related to the welfare of children, and an electronic journal, Child Welfare Review, a library, a resource on issues related to sources on child welfare. It also features a directory of email addresses for social work faculty.

Child Welfare League of America

http://www.cwla.org/

The Child Welfare League of America is the nation's oldest and largest organization devoted entirely to the well-being of America's vulnerable children and their families. The site provides information about the CWLA, advocacy tips, action alerts, and child welfare statistics.

part

2

Children Now

http://www.childrennow.org/

Children Now is a nonpartisan, independent voice for children, working to translate the nation's commitment to children and families into action. The site provides access to Children Now publications, poll results, policy papers, press materials, action updates on federal and state legislation, and links to other Web sites devoted to children's issues. Users who subscribe to Children Now's Internet Digest receive online updates on children's issues.

Children's Defense Fund

http://www.childrensdefense.org/

The Children's Defense Fund exists to provide a strong and effective voice for all the children of America, who cannot vote, lobby, or speak for themselves. The site provides information about the activities of the CDF, issues, news and reports, the Black Community Crusade for Children, Stand for Children, and links to related resources.

Family.Com

http://family.disney.com/

From Disney Online, Family.com is a service for parents offering comprehensive, high-quality, customizable information for raising children. Glitzy, but worth a visit.

National 4-H Council

http://www.fourhcouncil.edu/

National 4-H Council is a not-for-profit educational organization devoted to creating exciting programs and opportunities for young people. The site presents information about the organization and its activities.

National Parent Information Network

http://npin.org/

The purpose of NPIN is to provide information to parents and those who work with parents and to foster the exchange of parenting materials.

National Youth Center Network

http://www.leap.yale.edu/nycn/dir/biglist.html

An annotated list of online resources for youth organizations. Topics include the environment, family/parents/caregivers, health, human resources/services, institutions/museums, k-12 general, mathematics, networks, science, and special education/special needs.

PARENTS PLACE.COM

http://www.parentsplace.com/

The first parenting community on the Web. Provides parenting literature, advice columns, chat, bulletin boards, and shopping.

State of the World's Children—1996

http://www.unicef.org/sowc96/

UNICEF's 50th anniversary site presents a snapshot of the world's children in 1996, including children in war, statistical tables, regional spotlights, and references.

YouthNet

`http://www.youthnet.org.uk/`

This UK site provides a wealth of information for youths about everything ranging from relationships to housing, and with links to virtually any subject which conceivably could be of interest to adolescents.

YO! Youth Outlook

`http://www.pacificnews.org/yo/`

YO! (YOUTH OUTLOOK) is a bi-monthly news-journal of youth culture produced by young people in the San Francisco Bay Area for Pacific News Service. The Web page features selected contents.

Youth and Children Resources Net

`http://www.child.net/`

Maintained by the National Children's Coalition with sponsorship from Streetcats Foundation, this page aspires to be a megasite. It provides links to news, information, resources and referrals for and about kids and teens on the World Wide Web.

part
2

CLINICAL SOCIAL WORK PRACTICE

APsa: The American Psychoanalytic Association

`http://www.apsa.org/`

Home page of the American Psychoanalytic Association.

Behavior Analysis

`http://www.coedu.usf.edu/behavior/`

The main purpose of this home page is to provide a low-response cost outlet to some of the interesting things that are available on the Internet relating to behavior analysis.

Behaviour Analysis

`http://server.bmod.athabascau.ca/html/aupr/ba.htm`

Maintained by Athabasca University, this is believed to be the largest list of Web-based behavior-analysis resources on the Internet.

Behavior OnLine

http://www.behavior.net/

Behavior OnLine aspires to be the meeting place online for Mental Health and Applied Behavioral Science professionals. It hosts ongoing discussions on a variety of therapeutic approaches and provides links to organizations and interests groups and to other resources.

Cognitive Therapy

http://mindstreet.com/

MindStreet is a multimedia learning program which uses full-screen, full-motion video and consists of 5–8 hours of computer-assisted psychotherapy, plus a take-home manual with customized homework assignments for each patient. The program uses cognitive strategies for treating depression.

Counseling Center University at Buffalo

http://ub-counseling.buffalo.edu/

The Counseling Center Self-Help Home Page presents a wide selection of documents, Internet resources, referrals, and reading lists, all to help students with day-to-day stresses and difficult periods in their lives.

FreudNet: The A. A. Brill Library

http://www.interport.net/nypsan/

This server provides access to information about library services and the collection, as well as general information about psychoanalysis within the New York area and around the country.

Gestalt Therapy

http://www.gestalt.org/

The Gestalt Therapy Page, the Internet resource center for Gestalt therapy, includes a world-wide directory of Gestalt therapists, a Gestalt bibliography, a News at Notes bulletin board, and articles relating to Gestalt therapy.

GrassRoots

http://www.enabling.org/grassroots/

GrassRoots is an online, text-based, virtual reality community, MOO, where people from around the world can come together for support, education, and fun. This online community is being designed to accommodate the needs of persons with disabilities. GrassRoots has been created in the Multi-user Object Oriented (MOO) programming language that has two components, allowing the creation of an accessible site that is uniquely effective for social interaction and education.

The National Institute for the Psychotherapies

`http://www.nipinst.org/`

The National Institute for the Psychotherapies (NIP) training programs enhance the capacity of mental health professionals to treat child, adolescent and adult clients. The training reflects a unique commitment to draw on a wide range of theories of psychotherapy, to support the integration of existing treatment modalities, and to develop new treatment approaches.

NetPsych.com

`http://netpsych.com/`

This site explores the new uses of the Internet to deliver Psychological and Healthcare Services. NetPsych is the first site to focus exclusively on online resources. "HUH?" is a great button.

Psychotherapy on the Internet

`http://www.nyreferrals.com/psychotherapy/`

This Web site is intended as a guide to the understanding the "how" and "why" of psychotherapy services being offered, wholly and in part, on the Internet. It provides an extensive reading list of online resources, journals and books. There is also a discussion area and guest book for those who want to comment, discuss, or ask questions.

Support Coalition: Human Rights and Psychiatry Home Page

`http://www.efn.org/~dendron/`

The Support Coalition is dedicated to exposing human rights abuses by the psychiatry profession.

part

2

COMMUNITY ORGANIZATIONS

Campus Outreach Opportunity League

`http://www.COOL2SERVE.org/`

Founded in 1984, the Campus Outreach Opportunity League (COOL) is a national nonprofit that helps college students start, strengthen, and expand their community service programs.

The Center for Civic Networking

`http://www.civic.net:2401/ccn.html`

The Center for Civic Networking (CCN) is a nonprofit organization dedicated to applying information infrastructure to the broad public good—particularly by putting information infrastructure to work within local communities to improve delivery of local government services, improving access to information that people need in order to function as informed citizens, broadening citizen participation in governance, and stimulating economic and community development. Among the topics covered on the site are issues related to community building on the Internet and Internet access for the poor.

CivicNet

`http://development.civicnet.org/civicnet/`

The Center for Civic Networking promotes best practices and policies that foster the public use of information infrastructure for community economic development, social service delivery and participation in governance.

The Community Builders Fellowship

`http://www.hud.gov/cb/cbsplash.html`

A program of the US Department of Housing and Urban Development, in partnership with Harvard University's John F. Kennedy School of Government, the purpose of the Community Builders Fellowship program to educate and train individuals from diverse professions as Community Builders. As Community Builders, individuals can obtain practical, hands-on experience in community and economic development during a two-to-four year stay with HUD.

Community Networking Resources

http://www.nlc-bnc.ca/ifla/II/commun.htm

This site offers links to a variety of Internet resources related to Internet access and community-building.

Community Networks: An Online Guide to Resources

http://mason.gmu.edu/~pbaker/1cnindex.html

This Web site is a compilation of references, links, and publications related to a variety of networked information infrastructures.

HandsNet

http://www.handsnet.org/

HandsNet is a national, nonprofit organization that promotes information sharing, cross-sector collaboration and advocacy among individuals and organizations working on a broad range of public interest issues.

part

2

How to Use the Internet for Organizing

http://www.nonviolence.org/support/

Martin Kelley, of The Nonviolence Web, has compiled "How to Use the Internet for Organizing" that can be useful to almost any organization.

The Human SERVE Home Page

http://www.igc.apc.org/humanserve/

This site reports on the Campaign for Universal Voter Registration, and offers statistical information related to voter registration, community organization manuals, and reports on legal challenges to the motor/voter bill.

Idealist

http://www.idealist.org/

Idealist is a fully interactive system that enables any nonprofit or community organization— whether it has a Web site or not—to enter and update detailed information about its services, volunteer opportunities, internships, job openings, upcoming events, and any material or publication it has produced. 14,000 organizations in 125 countries are already using Idealist.

National Urban League

`http://www.nul.org`

The mission of the National Urban League is to assist African Americans in the achievement of social and economic equality. The Board of Trustees of the National Urban League and all of its affiliates reflect a diverse body of community, government, and corporate leaders. The League implements its mission through advocacy, bridge building, program services, and research.

Neighborhoods Online

`http://www.libertynet.org/nol/natl.html`

Neighborhoods Online was created in 1995 by the Institute for the Study of Civic Values and Philadelphia's LibertyNet as an online resource center for people working to build strong communities throughout the United States. Their aim is to provide fast access to information and ideas covering all aspects of neighborhood revitalization, as well as to create a national network of neighborhood activists. The site offers information related to community development, education, crime, jobs, environment, health, and human services.

NetAction Internet Resources

`http://www.netaction.org/resources.html`

This is a wonderful list of annotated links. Virtually everything you need to know to be a community activist using the Internet.

Nurturing Neighborhood Nets

`http://web.mit.edu/techreview/www/articles/oct97/`
`chapman .html`

Interesting article about how providing free access to computer networking can extend the pleasures and benefits of the Net to people living in poor communities. Provides links to several community organization efforts utilizing Internet resources.

part
2

People-Link

`http://www.People-Link.com/`

People Link provides integrated communications to the progressive, socially responsible business, and organized labor communities. The site offers progressive and alternative news media, labor union sites and information, links to socially responsible businesses, information on environmental issues, left wing activities, women, gays and lesbians, people of color, and progressive arts.

Social Contract Project

`http://www.libertynet.org/edcivic/sochome.html`

Through the Social Contract Project, the Institute for the Study of Civic Values has developed a new way for neighborhood activists, business leaders, and public officials to develop comprehensive plans for neighborhood improvement. These stakeholders negotiate an explicit social contract defining how they will work together to make the neighborhood is clean, safe, economically viable, and a decent place to raise children. The site details the work of the project.

part
2

DISABILITIES

Ability

`http://www.ability.org.uk`

Ability is a grassroots organization in the UK which is dedicated to utilizing computer technology and the Internet for people with disabilities. The site offers access to disability and health resources, social contacts, message boards, classified ads, and news.

Active Living Alliance

`http://activeliving.ca/activeliving/alliance/alliance .html`

The Active Living Alliance for Canadians with a Disability is a partnership of 17 National Associations whose common goal is to facilitate active living opportunities for Canadians with a disability. Information about the alliance, news, and links to related resources are offered.

ADA Information Center On-Line Web Site

http://www.idir.net/~adabbs/

Sponsored by the Kansas Commission on Disability Concerns, this site offers a wealth of information and resources for people with disabilities in Kansas, nationally and internationally.

American Council for the Blind

http://www.acb.org/

This site offers information about the activities of the organization, recent issues of its monthly publications, and helpful resources and information about blindness.

American Foundation for the Blind

http://www.afb.org/

part
2

Information about the AFB, the Journal of Visual Impairment and Blindness, the AFB Press Catalog, the Helen Keller photograph collection, and information on blindness, low vision and related issues.

The Archimedes Project

http://www-csli.stanford.edu/arch/

The mission of the Archimedes Project is to help secure equality of access to information for individuals with disabilities through the development of computer technology and the promulgation of knowledge about disability to present and future designers in academia and industry.

The ARC

http://TheArc.org

The Arc (formerly Association for Retarded Citizens of the United States) is the country's largest voluntary organization committed to the welfare of all children and adults with mental retardation and their families.

Associated Services for the Blind

http://www.libertynet.org/asbinfo/

This site offers information about the organization's services and information about subscribing to popular national magazines on cassette. The Web site is offered in an all audio version.

The Center for Independent Living

http://www.cilberkeley.org/

The Center for Independent Living (CIL) is a national leader in helping people with disabilities live independently and become productive, fully participating members of society.

disABILITY Information and Resources

http://www.eskimo.com/~jlubin/disabled.html

One of the largest collections of resources for all types of disabilities.

Disability and Rehabilitation Resources on the Web

http://www.educ.state.ak.us/VocRehab/govscomm/
rehab.html

This Web resource is a project of the Alaska Governor's Committee on Employment and Rehabilitation of People with Disabilities. It provides links to a variety of resources across the United States.

Disabled Peoples' International

http://www.dpi.org

The purpose of DPI is to promote the Human Rights of People with Disabilities through full participation, equalization of opportunity and development. DPI is a grassroots, cross-disability network with member organizations in over 110 countries, over half of which are in the developing world. DPI is administrated through the headquarters in Winnipeg, Canada and through eight Regional Development Offices. DPI has consultative status with the ECOSOC, UNESCO, WHO, and the ILO, and has official observer status at the United Nations General Assembly.

Down Syndrome WWW Page

http://www.nas.com/downsyn/

part
2

A support and information page for parents, professionals and others interested in Down syndrome.

Dyslexia Archive

http://www.hensa.ac.uk/dyslexia.html

The Dyslexia Archive is an ever growing collection of up-to-date material covering all aspects of dyslexia.

ERIC Clearinghouse on Disabilities and Gifted Education

http://www.cec.sped.org/er-menu.htm

ERIC EC is part of the National Library of Education (NLE), Office of Educational Research and Improvement (OERI), U.S. Department of Education. It is operated by The Council for Exceptional Children (CEC). ERIC EC provides information on the education of individuals with disabilities as well as those who are gifted.

Gallaudet Research Institute

http://gri.gallaudet.edu/

Gallaudet University is the world's only four-year university for deaf and hard of hearing undergraduate students. The Gallaudet Research Institute specializes in research about the deaf.

Hattie Larlham Foundation

http://www.larlham.org/

HLF is a private, nonprofit service agency for young people with mental retardation, developmental disabilities and/or complex medical needs. The Web site is offered as a service for the families of children with profound disabilities, professionals who work with children having disabilities and anyone who wishes to learn more.

Hearing Loss Resources

http://www.webcom.com/~houtx/

The SayWhatClub sponsors the Hearing Loss Resources Web site. Internet Mailing lists and nonprofit organizations that focus on the issue of hearing loss are featured.

part
2

International Center for Disablity Resources on the Internet—Home Page

http://www.icdri.org/

The Center's mission is to collect and present as many disability-related Internet resources as there are available, including resources directly related to disabilities and other resources that may be helpful to the disability community. These resources are presented in a manner that is accessible to a wide and varied audience. The Center's scope is international.

Language Based Learning Disability

http://www-ld.ucsf.edu/

The University of California at San Francisco offers this site as a compendium of information on resources for the remediation of language-based disabilities.

National Federation of the Blind

http://www.nfb.org/

The goal of the NFB involves the removal of legal, economic, and social discriminations; the education of the public to new concepts concerning blindness; and the achievement by all blind people of the right to exercise to the fullest their individual talents and capacities.

part

2

National Institute for Life Planning

http://www.sonic.net/nilp/

NILP is a national organization dedicated to promoting transition, life and person centered planning for all persons with disabilities and their families. The site provides families with information on government benefits, advocacy, guardianship, aging, housing, and supported employment.

National Library Service for the Blind and Physically Handicapped

http://lcweb.loc.gov/nls/

The Library of Congress a free library program of Braille and recorded materials circulated to eligible borrowers through a network of cooperating libraries. This Web site offers access to online catalogs of holdings.

National Technical Institute for the Deaf

`http://www.isc.rit.edu/~418www/`

One of the seven colleges of the Rochester Institute of Technology (RIT), NTID is the world's first and largest technological college for deaf students. It represents the first concerted effort to educate large numbers of deaf students within a college campus planned principally for hearing students.

Shriver Center

`http://www.shriver.org/`

The Eunice Kennedy Shriver Center for Mental Retardation, Inc. is a not-for-profit service, training and research institute. The site offers information about their research, training, and services divisions.

Values into Action

`http://www.demon.co.uk/via`

VIA is a nonprofit organization which works to promote the rights of people with learning difficulties. The site offers information to promote the civil rights of people with disabilities.

World Information on Disability

`http://www.dais.is.tohoku.ac.jp/~iwan/foreign_res.html`

This is a Japanese site which pulls together a variety of resources on disabilities.

DIVERSITY

The African World Community Network

`http://www.he.net/~awe/`

Links to Afrocentric resources around the Internet.

Asian American Resources

`http://www.mit.edu:8001/afs/athena.mit.edu/user/i/r/i rie/www/aa r.html`

Provides a variety of links to Internet resources about Asian Americans.

part **2**

Asian Studies WWW Monitor

http://coombs.anu.edu.au/asia-www-monitor.html

This online newsletter was established to provide resources which are inspected and rated in terms of the quality, overall reliability and usefulness of their content to the social sciences' research in Asia–Pacific region.

The Amistad Research Center

http://www.tmc.tulane.edu/researchadmin/arc.htm

An independent archives, library, and museum dedicated to preserving African-American and ethnic history and culture, housed at Tulane University.

The African American Home Page

http://www.lainet.com/~joejones/

Links to African American resources, including one of the largest collections of African American art on the Internet. Also includes recipes, bulletin boards, library resources, and links to related sites.

The Chicano/Latino Electronic Network

http://latino.sscnet.ucla.edu/

CLNet is an emerging digital library on Latinas/os in the United States and a joint project of the Center for Virtual Research in the College of Humanities, Arts, and Social Sciences at the UC Riverside, the Chicano Studies Research Library at UCLA and the Linguistic Minority Research Institute at the UC Santa Barbara.

The Cradleboard Teaching Project

http://www.cradleboard.org/

Founded by Buffy Sainte-Marie, the Nihewan Foundation is dedicated to the development of curricula for American Indian Education. Included in this site is a comprehensive listing of links to Tribal resources across North America.

part
2

CyberMuslim Information Collective

http://www.uum.edu.my/~masjid/bina.htm

This site contains a comprehensive listing of Muslim resources available on the Internet.

Institute of Hispanic-Latino Cultures

http://www.ufsa.ufl.edu/lacasita/

Offers information for students at the University of Florida.

The Jewish Communication Network

http://www.jcn18.com/

An online center serving information for families, teachers, writers, Jewish professionals and organizations from around the world.

part
2

LATIF.com Home

http://www.latif.com/

A listing of links and informational resources about Islam.

Latin-American Network Information Center

http://info.lanic.utexas.edu/

This site is considered by some to be by far the best online resource for information about Latin America and the Caribbean.

Latino Link

http://www.latinolink.com/

Considered by some to be the premiere spot for Latinos on the Web. News, chat, job bank, weekly email newsletter, bulletin boards and more.

Minority Rights Group International

http://www.minorityrights.org/

MRG is an international non governmental organization working to secure justice for minorities and majorities suffering discrimination and prejudice and to active the peaceful coexistence of majority and minority communities. MRG informs and warns governments, the international community, non governmental organizations and the wider public about the situation of minorities around the world.

National Congress of American Indians

http://www.cwis.org/ncai.html

Sponsored by the Center For World Indigenous Studies and the Fourth World Documentation Project. This project is an online library of texts which record and preserve Indian struggles to regain their rightful place in the international community.

Native American Home Pages

http://www.pitt.edu/~lmitten/indians.html

A wealth of links to Indian-focused Internet resources.

NetNoir

http://www.netnoir.com/

Your gateway to everything afrocentric, afro-latin, afro-caribbean, afro-european, continental african or african-american. chat, play games, or read articles.

Swagga.Com

http://www.swagga.com/afrolin.htm

This site represents a compendium of links to Internet resources for African Americans.

The Universal Black Pages

http://www.ubp.com/

The Universal Black Pages is an information service which resides at the Georgia Institute of Technology but is not affiliated with the Institute. The main purpose of the UBP is to have a complete and comprehensive listing of African Diaspora related Web pages at a central site.

part
2

UCI Southeast Asian Archive

http://pitcairn.lib.uci.edu/sea/seahome.html

The Archive, housed at University of California, Irvine Libraries, collects materials relating to the resettlement of Southeast Asian refugees and immigrants in the United States, the "boat people" and land refugees, and the culture and history of Cambodia, Laos, and Vietnam.

The UCLA Asian American Studies Center

http://www.sscnet.ucla.edu/aasc/

Highlights the activities of the center, provides access to publications, and links to related resources.

The WWW Hmong Homepage

http://www.stolaf.edu/people/cdr/hmong/

This is a collection of resources relating to Hmong history, culture, language, and current events. It is served by St. Olaf College.

part

2

GENDER

Bookbeast's Feminist Threads Homepage

http://users.aol.com/bookbeast/ft.htm

Offers a variety of information of interest to women, including U.S. politics, Ethnic and International resources, general and reference resources, books and publications, law and freedom, religion, lesbian culture, music, art and film, health and safety, work and leisure, and notices about upcoming events.

Feminism and Women's Resources

http://www.ibd.nrc.ca/~mansfield/feminism/

This is a listing of many of the feminism, women's studies, or women-related sources on the net.

Feminist Activist Resources

http://www.igc.org/women/feminist.html

This guide is particularly oriented toward connecting feminists who are activists to useful resources on the Internet.

Feminist.Com

`http://feminist.com/`

FEMINIST.COM is aimed at helping women network, and educating and empowering women (and men) on issues that affect their lives. Offers news, information about resources, activism, women's health, articles and speeches, women-owned businesses, and classifieds.

Feminist Majority Foundation

`http://www.feminist.org/`

The Feminist Majority and The Feminist Majority Foundation are committed to empowering women and winning equality through research, the sharing of information of value to feminists everywhere, and effective action. The site offers action alerts, news and press releases, and information about events of interest.

The Greenman

`http://www.greenman.org/`

The Greenman is a Web site dedicated to male spirituality and the issues common to men looking for more in theis lives.

The International Foundation for Gender Education

`http://www.ifge.org/`

The International Foundation for Gender Education (IFGE), founded in 1987, is a leading advocate and educational organization for promoting the self-definition and free expression of individual gender identity.

Men's Issues Page

`http://www.vix.com/men/`

The mission of this site is to cover the several men's movements encyclopediacally. It seeks to maintain comprehensive reference lists of mens movement organizations, books, periodicals, Web links and other related

part

2

resources, as well as to serve as an online reference source for statistics, studies and bibliographies of interest to the mens movements.

Men's Movement Resources on the Web

http://www.psychstat.smsu.edu/scripts/dws148f/
mensresourcesmain.asp

David W. Stockburger has compiled a list of resources for men's issues, including organizations, literature and information, advocacy pages, and government links.

National Organization for Women

http://now.org/

Official home page of the National Organization for Women. Offers information about the organization and its agenda, as well as feminism, women, abortion rights, violence against women, racial and ethnic diversity, and economic equity.

Virtual Sisterhood

http://www.igc.apc.org/vsister/

Virtual Sisterhood is a global women's electronic support network dedicated to strengthening and magnifying the impact of feminist organizing through promotion of electronic communications use within the global women's movement.

Women.com

http;//www.women.com

A women's network for women's content and community, includes Women's Wire, Beatrice's Web Guide, Prevention's Healthy Ideas, Stork Site, and MoneyMode, plus community forums where our visitors take center stage.

Women's Resource Center

http://www.Colorado.EDU/WomensResourceCenter/

The Women's Resource Center at the University of Colorado, Boulder serves as a resource for the university community and an advocate for women of all backgrounds, races, classes, ages, sexual orientations, political and religious beliefs, and physical abilities.

Women's Resources on the Web: INDEX

`http://www.polaris.net/~ratliff/emily/women.html`

Offers links related to health, safety, sexuality, sports, Women's Studies, women in technology, politics and activism, and more.

WWWomen!

`http://www.wwwomen.com/`

Considered to be the premier search directory for women's resources on the Internet, offers both hierarchical and keyword searching.

HEALTH

American Public Health Association

`http://www.apha.org/`

APHA represents more than 50,000 members from over 50 occupations of public health, bringing together researchers, health service providers, administrators, teachers, and other health workers in a unique, multidisciplinary environment of professional exchange, study, and action.

AMSO Managed Care Forum

`http://www.amso.com/`

Home page for American Medical Specialty Organization Managed Care Forum and other related health care issues. The World-Wide Healthcare Poll and Healthcare forums provide a place for the health care professional, executive, or a concerned health care consumer to read and submit ideas and information in a moderated environment.

Attention Deficit Disorder

`http://www.pilgrims.net/plymouth/schools/Links/SPED/
ADD.html`

A project of the Plymouth, Massachusetts public schools, this page provides a wealth of Internet resources related to attention deficit disorder.

part
2

The Canadian Health Network

http://www.hc-sc.gc.ca/

Information about the health care system in Canada and links to informational resources.

CancerWEB

http://www.graylab.ac.uk/cancernet/

This cancer resource site has information available on many different aspects of cancer investigation and treatment. Especially helpful is an online medical dictionary.

Center for Health Education

http://www.statpath.com

Center for Health Education is a nonprofit organization providing innovative resources to help clinicians manage patient care in a capitated, managed care environment.

Center for Rural Health and Social Service Development

http://www.siu.edu/~crhssd/

Southern Illinois University at Carbondale's CRHSSD conducts research, needs assessments, demonstration projects, program evaluations, and training; tests new models of health care delivery; and develops policy recommendations to improve the health of our rural population.

ChronicILLNet

http://www.chronicillnet.org/

This is the first multimedia information source on the Internet dedicated to chronic illnesses including AIDS, cancer, Persian Gulf War Syndrome, autoimmune diseases, Chronic Fatigue Syndrome, heart disease and neurological diseases. This site offers information for researchers, patients, lay people, and physicians.

Clinical Trials Listings

http://www.CenterWatch.com/

part
2

The CenterWatch Clinical Trials Listing Service is an international listing of clinical research trials. The site enables for clinical trials, for information about physicians and medical centers performing clinical research, and to learn about drug therapies newly approved by the Food and Drug Administration.

Diabetes Home Page

`http://www.cdc.gov/nccdphp/ddt/`

Sponsored by the Division of Diabetes Translation, a division of the National Center for Chronic Disease Prevention and Health Promotion of the Centers for Disease Control and Prevention. The division is responsible for translating scientific research findings into health promotion, disease prevention and treatment strategies.

Drug Database

`http://pharminfo.com/drugdb/`

A database of information on prescription drugs, searchable by generic or trade name.

part

2

Go Ask Alice!

`http://www.goaskalice.columbia.edu/`

Sponsored by Healthwise, the Health Education and Wellness program of the Columbia University Health Service, *Go Ask Alice!* is an interactive question and answer service, answering questions each week about health, including questions about sexuality, sexual health, relationships, general health, fitness and nutrition, emotional well-being, and alcohol and other drugs.

healthfinder

`http://www.healthfinder.org/`

healthfinder™is a gateway consumer health and human services information Web site from the United States government. healthfinder™can lead you to selected online publications, clearinghouses, databases, Web sites, and support and self-help groups, as well as the government agencies and not-for-profit organizations that produce reliable information for the public. Launched in April 1997, healthfinder™served Internet users over 1.7 million times in its first year online.

Juvenile Diabetes Foundation

http://www.jdfcure.org/

The Juvenile Diabetes Foundation is a not-for-profit, voluntary health agency whose mission is to support and fund research to find a cure for diabetes and its complications. The site offers a range of diabetes information.

Med Help International

http://medhlp.netusa.net/

Med Help International is dedicated to helping all who are in need find qualified medical information and support for their medical conditions and questions, regardless of their economic status or geographic location. Offers library searches and patient support through chat resources.

part
2

The Minority Health Network

http://www.pitt.edu/~ejb4/min/

MHNet is a World Wide Web based information source for individuals interested in the health of minority groups, referring to all people of color and people who are underrepresented economically and socially.

Muscular Dystrophy Association

http://www.mdausa.org

Offers links to information about MD and to related associations worldwide.

National Center for Farmworker Health

http://www.ncfh.org

NCFH is a private, not-for-profit corporation located in Austin, Texas. NCFH has evolved into a multi-faceted organization which provides a wide range of services dedicated to improving the health of the workers who harvest America's crops.

Nursing Net

http://www.nursingnet.org/

NursingNet's mission is to help further the knowledge and understanding of Nursing for the public, and to provide a forum for medical professionals and students to obtain and disseminate information about nursing and medically related subjects. Offers a wide range of Internet nursing resources.

On-line Resources for Diabetics

http://www.cruzio.com/~mendosa/faq.htm

This Web page brings together in one place descriptions of and links to all those places where diabetics can find resources that they can use.

PEDINFO Home Page

http://www.pedinfo.org/

This Web server is dedicated to the dissemination of online information for pediatricians and others interested in child health.

part

2

National Information Center on Health Services Research

http://www.nlm.nih.gov/nichsr/

NICHSR was created at the National Library of to improve the collection, storage, analysis, retrieval, and dissemination of information on health services research, clinical practice guidelines, and on health care technology, including the assessment of such technology.

Pediatric Points of Interest

http://www.med.jhu.edu/peds/neonatology/poi.html

Sponsored by Johns Hopkins University, the Pediatric Points of Interest page is a searchable collection of links to resources in Pediatrics and Child Health.

Synapse Publishing

http://www.medlib.com/

Synapse, Inc. creates computerized decision support systems for physicians and other health care professionals. They are the publishers of the

Cochrane Database of Systematic Reviews, Stroke: A Practical Guide to Management (Blackwell), and creators of the StrokeNet and the Stroke Guidance System. Their site offers some great resources about neuro-muscular illnesses.

Viaticus

http://www.vrsc.com/process.htm

Information about using life insurance policies to pay medical bills, to supplement income, or to relieve other financial burdens for people with a life-threatening illness.

WWW Virtual Library: Biosciences: Medicine

http://www.ohsu.edu/cliniweb/wwwvl/

An hierarchical listing of medical topics for finding resources on the Web.

Y-Me National Breast Cancer Organization

http://www.y-me.org/

Y-ME National Breast Cancer Organization has a commitment to provide information and support to anyone who has been touched by breast cancer. Y-ME serves women with breast cancer and their families and friends through their national hotline, open door groups, early detection workshops and local chapters.

HIV/AIDS

ACSN—AIDS Caregivers Support Network

http://www.wolfenet.com/~acsn/

ACSN is a nonprofit organization dedicated to assisting AIDS caregivers with emotional and practical support through group services, individual support, and written materials. The site provides information about the organization, Circles of Care, a quarterly newsletter, and other resources on the Web.

ACT-UP NY

http://www.actupny.org/

The New York chapter of this advocacy and political action group's home page provides information about the organization, links, and an activist e-mail list signup.

AIDS Project—Los Angeles

http://www.apla.org/

Uses a search engine to link users to a variety of information, including services, special events, volunteer opportunities, publications, grass roots organizing, and information links.

AIDS Resource List

http://www.teleport.com/~celinec/aids.shtml

A comprehensive list of HIV/AIDS related links from Celine Chamberlin, a self-proclaimed Internet addict.

The Body: A Multimedia AIDS and HIV Resource

http://www.thebody.com/

Covers many topics, including: prevention, safe sex, testing, treatment (protease inhibitors, combination therapy, viral load, azt, ddi, ddc, d4t, 3tc, reverse transcriptase), QandA w/ experts, hotlines, and politics.

part 2

Center for AIDS Prevention Studies

http://www.epibiostat.ucsf.edu/capsweb/

CAPS is committed to maintaining a focus on prevention of HIV disease, using the expertise of multiple disciplines, and an applied and community-based perspective within a university setting. The Web site features information about the activities of the center, fact sheets, and a "Prevention Toolbox."

Children with AIDS Project

http://www.aidskids.org/

Children with AIDS Project of America offers a variety of services for children infected/affected by AIDS or drug exposed infants who will require foster or adoptive families. The site offers information about the organization and links to other resources.

Clinical Care Options for HIV

http://www.healthcg.com/

HIV education and treatment info site offering free online interactive CME programs for healthcare professionals, online journal, next day summaries of major HIV meetings.

Correctional HIV Consortium (CHC)

http://www.silcom.com/~chc/

Nonprofit corporation whose area of expertise is AIDS and HIV disease as it affects the various components of the criminal justice system and corrections communities.

Detroit Community AIDS Library

http://www.libraries.wayne.edu/dcal/aids.html

part

2

Gateway to HIV/AIDS Information for Detroit and Southeastern Michigan. Provides links to news and announcements, local AIDS service organizations, searchable databases, and HIV/AIDS Internet resources.

HIV InSite

http://hivinsite.ucsf.edu/

Comprehensive and reliable information on HIV/AIDS treatment, policy, research, epidemiology, and prevention from the University of California, San Francisco.

HIV Law

http://www.hivlawtoday.com/

Presented by Paul Hampton Crockett., this site represents a comprehensive survival guide to the legal system for people living with HIV.

HIVpositive.com

http://www.hivpositive.com/

The HIVpositive site offers HIV-related info on a wide-range of topics including but not limited to nutrition, treatment, caregivers, finances, and drug advisories. The mission of the site is to improve the quality of life of anyone affected in some way by the HIV virus. Among the agencies contributing information are the CDC, FDA NIH, the Gay Men's Health Crisis, and the American Foundation for AIDS Research.

HIV/AIDS Treatment Information

http://www.hivatis.org/

The HIV/AIDS Treatment Information Service (ATIS) provides timely, accurate treatment information on HIV and AIDS through the use of federally approved treatment guidelines and information. The HSTAT database contains the full text of approved treatment guidelines being used by the service.

International Council of AIDS Service Organizations

http://www.web.apc.org/~icaso/icaso.html

The ICASO network is an interactive global focus point in the international HIV/AIDS world, gathering and disseminating information and analysis on key issues, coordinating the development of CBO/NGO positions on these issues, and working as partners with key international agencies to ensure that the concerns and interests of CBOs and NGOs around the world are articulated and represented at all levels.

part

2

Marty Howard's HIV/AIDS HomePage

http://www.smartlink.net/~martinjh/

This page is designed to help users find as much HIV/AIDS related information as possible from one starting place.

Medscape—AIDS

http://www.medscape.com/Home/Topics/AIDS/AIDS.html

Medscape features peer-reviewed articles, zoomable color graphics, self-assessment features, medical information, medical news, free MEDLINE, CME credit, and annotated links to Internet resources.

MedWeb: AIDS and HIV

http://www.gen.emory.edu/medweb/medweb.aids.html

A service of Emery University Health Sciences Center Library, this site is one of the more complete lists of research references on HIV/AIDS available.

National Centre for HIV Social Research

http://www.bhs.mq.edu.au/nchsr/

This site documents the research activities of this Australian center.

Pets Are Loving Support

http://www.sonic.net/~pals/

PALS is a nonprofit agency organized to improve the quality of life of people with AIDS by preserving and promoting the human/animal bond through the care and maintenance of their animal companions.

The Safer Sex Page

http://safersex.org/

A resource site providing information about safer sex, condoms, HIV, contraception, a forum, counselor information, and links to other resources.

SWEAIDS-NET

http://www.mun.ca/sweaids/sweaids.html

HIV/AIDS Social Work Education Canadian Network. The site serves as an interactive tool for sharing experiences, resources, and information social work educators, field instructors, students and trainers involved in HIV/AIDS related social work.

UNAIDS

http://www.unaids.org

The Joint United Nations Programme on HIV/AIDS maintains this page to disseminate information on HIV/AIDS.

www.aidsnyc.org

http://www.aidsnyc.org/

A linked collection of pages from HIV/AIDS community based organizations in New York City.

HOUSING, HUNGER, AND POVERTY

Action Aid

http://www.oneworld.org/actionaid/

ACTIONAID is a leading development charity working directly with three million of the world's poorest people in Africa, Asia and Latin America, helping them in their fight against poverty.

America's Charities

http://www.charities.org/

America's Charities goal is to provide member charities with the necessary resources to meet needs impacting human service, health and education, civil and human rights, and the environment.

Bread for the World

http://www.bread.org/

Citizens' movement seeking justice for the world's hungry people by lobbying our nation's decision makers.

Education of Homeless Children and Youth

http://nch.ari.net/edchild.html

Fact sheet from the National Coalition for the Homeless.

Food For The Hungry: World Crisis Network

http://www.fh.org/

Food for the Hungry feeds the hungry world-wide. This Internet site also includes Gopher, FTP, majordomo/listserv services. A MUD/MOO environment is also under construction.

Food Research and Action Center

http://www.frac.org/

FRAC works to improve public policies to eradicate hunger and undernutrition in the United States.

part

2

HomeAid America

http://www.HomeAid.org/

HomeAid's mission is to build or renovate shelters for transitionally homeless men, women and children. HomeAid was created to help National Association of Home Builders—affiliated home building associations develop their own independently operated HomeAid programs to help fulfill the HomeAid mission across the nation. The site offers links to a wealth of housing-related information resources.

Homeless in America

http://www.commnet.edu/QVCTC/student/GaryOKeefe/homeless/frame.html

Information page on who are homeless in America and why they are homeless. There is also information about support groups for the homeless and political advocacy.

Homelessness

http://aspe.os.dhhs.gov/progsys/homeless/

Offers information about homelessness in America as well as about U.S. Department of Health and Human Services assistance programs, publications, research results, and other resources.

Hunger Notes

http://www.brown.edu/Departments/World_Hunger_Program/hungerweb/HN/HNHomePg.html

Hunger Notes is an online journal which is sponsored by the World Hunger Education Service. Its mission is to inform the community of people interested in issues of hunger and poverty, the public, and policy-makers, about the causes, extent, and efforts to end hunger and poverty in the United States and the world; to promote further understanding which integrates ethical, religious, social, economic, political, and scientific perspectives on hunger and poverty; to facilitate communication and networking among those who are working for solutions; and to promote individual and collective commitment to solutions to the hunger and poverty which confront hundreds of millions of the people of the world.

HungerWeb

http://www.brown.edu/Departments/World_Hunger_
Program/

A project of the World Hunger Program, HungerWeb aims to help prevent and eradicate hunger by facilitating the free exchange of ideas and information regarding the causes of, and solutions to, hunger.

Institute for Research on Poverty (IRP)

http://www.ssc.wisc.edu/irp/

IRP provides online publications and extensive links to poverty-related statistics and information sources.

Joint Center for Poverty Research

http://www.jcpr.org/

The Northwestern University / University of Chicago Joint Center for Poverty Research is a national and interdisciplinary community of researchers whose work advances the understanding of what it means to be poor and live in America.

part
2

Luxembourg Income Study

http://lissy.ceps.lu/

The Luxembourg Income Study has four goals: (1) to test the feasibility of creating a database containing social and economic data collected in household surveys from different countries; (2) provide a method allowing researchers to use the data under restrictions required by the countries providing the data; (3) create a system that will allow research requests to be received and returned to users at remote locations; and (4) promote comparative research on the economic status of populations in different countries.

National Center for Children in Poverty

http://cpmcnet.columbia.edu/dept/nccp/

The mission of the National Center for Children in Poverty is to identify and promote strategies that reduce the number of young children living in poverty in the United States, and that improve the life chances of the millions of children under six who a re growing up poor. Center projects concentrate on early childhood care and education; child and family health; family and community support; cross-cutting, multistate policy analyses; demographic and evaluation research; and communications.

National Coalition for the Homeless

http://nch.ari.net/

The National Coalition for the Homeless is a national advocacy network of homeless persons, activists, service providers, and others committed to ending homelessness through public education, policy advocacy, grass-roots organizing, and technical assistance.

National Health Care for the Homeless Council, Inc.

http://www.nashville.net/~hch/

Membership organization of health care providers working to help bring about reform of the health care system to best serve the needs of people who are homeless.

Northwest Harvest

http://www.blarg.net/~nharvest/

Northwest Harvest collects and distributes food to approximately 280 hunger programs in Washington State without tax dollars or fees of any kind. In an average month, 500,000 services are provided to individuals and families in need. Nearly half of these services go to children.

Poverty and Sustainable Livelihoods

http://www.undp.org/undp/seped/

Research, statistics and publications on poverty and sustainable livelihoods from the United Nations Development Programme.

Real Change

http://www.realchangenews.org/

Real Change is a newspaper for the homeless of Seattle, Washington. Highlights of recent issues are featured on this page.

RESULTS: Ending hunger and poverty

`http://action.org`

RESULTS is a nonprofit, grassroots citizen's lobby that identifies sustainable solutions to the problems of hunger and poverty, nationally and world-wide, and works to generate the resources necessary to make those solutions succeed. The site features information about the organization, action alerts, background on hunger and poverty issues, Capitol updates, articles about the organization, and links to other Web sites.

World Hunger Year

`http://www.iglou.com/why/`

Founded by Harry Chapin in 1975, WHY focuses attention on hunger and poverty and the grassroots initiatives that fight them.

MENTAL HEALTH

Alliance for Increased Mental Health Awareness

`http://views.vcu.edu/views/psych2/stigma.htm`

AIM-Awareness is a coalition of agencies, groups and individuals working to remove the stigma confronting people with mental illness.

At Health Home Page

`http://www.athealth.com/`

At Health provides mental health information, resources, a directory of licensed psychiatrists, psychologists, counselors and other therapists, and continuing education information.

Autism Resources

`http://web.syr.edu/~jmwobus/autism/`

This page is an organized list of resources about Autism that are available on the net.

part
2

Bereavement Resources

http://www.funeral.net/brvres.html

A variety of resources for mourners.

Cath's Eating Disorders Resources on Internet

http://www.stud.unit.no/studorg/ikstrh/ed/

This is a collection of links to various information on Eating Disorders all around the Net.

Children and Adults with Attention Deficit Disorder

http://www.chadd.org/

CH.A.D.D. is a nonprofit parent-based organization formed to better the lives of individuals with attention deficit disorders and those who care for them through family support and advocacy, public and professional education and encouragement of scientific research.

Crisis, Grief, and Healing

http://www.webhealing.com/

This page is meant to be a place men and women can browse to understand and honor the many different paths to heal strong emotions.

David Baldwin's Trauma Information Pages

http://www.trauma-pages.com/

The Trauma Information Pages focus primarily on emotional trauma and traumatic stress, including PTSD (Post-traumatic Stress Disorder), whether following individual traumatic experience(s) or a large-scale disaster. New information is added to this site about once a month. The purpose of this award-winning site is to provide information about traumatic stress for clinicians and researchers in the field.

Depression Resources List

http://www.execpc.com/~corbeau/

An updated list of Internet resources related to depression.

False Memory Syndrome Facts

`http://fmsf.org/`

This site offers pointers to key resources about "false memory syndrome," dissociation, delayed recall, repression, and recovered memories of child abuse and other traumatic events.

False Memory Syndrome Foundation

`http://advicom.com/~fitz/fmsf/`

The FMS Foundation is a nonprofit organization which is devoted to seeking the reasons for the spread of False Memory Syndrome; to working for the prevention of new cases of False Memory Syndrome; and to aiding the victims, both primary and secondary, of False Memory Syndrome.

GriefNet

`http://www.rivendell.org/`

Bereavement, grief, death and dying resources.

part
2

Institute of Psychiatry Library: Mental Health

`http://www.iop.bpmf.ac.uk/home/depts/library/ment.htm`

A very comprehensive list of links to resources in mental health.

The International Society for Mental Health Online

`http://www.ismho.org/`

The International Society for Mental Health Online (ISMHO) was formed in 1997 to promote the understanding, use and development of online communication, information and technology for the international mental health community.

Internet Mental Health Resources

`http://freenet.msp.mn.us/ip/stockley/mental_health.html`

Topical list of mental health links from Herbert D. Stockley.

Knowledge Exchange Network

http://www.mentalhealth.org/

KEN—the National Mental Health Services Knowledge Exchange Network—has an award-winning Web site that offers a wealth of information about mental health. Visitors can find a variety of mental health-related subjects from advocacy to Zoloft(TM), alternative care to managed care, anxiety disorders to statistics.

Louis de la Parte Florida Mental Health Institute

http://www.fmhi.usf.edu/

The state's primary research and training center for mental health services is recognized nationally for its innovative research and training. The site offers information about mental health needs and services in the state of Florida, and links to relevant information, including electronic publications.

MedWeb: Mental Health

http://www.gen.emory.edu/MEDWEB/keyword/mental_health
~psychiatry~psychology.html

Biomedical Internet resources from Emory University Health Sciences Center Library.

Mental Health Matters!

http://www.mental-health-matters.com/

Mental Health Matters! is a directory of mental health and mental illness information and resources for mental health professionals, patients, and families.

Mental Health Net

http://www.cmhc.com/

MHN considers itself the largest, most comprehensive guide to mental health online, featuring over 7,000 individual resources. This site, winner of several awards, covers information on disorders such as depression, anxiety, panic attacks, chronic fatigue syndrome and substance abuse, to professional resources in psychology, psychiatry and social work, journals, and self-help magazines.

The Mining Company Mental Health Resources

`http://mentalhealth.miningco.com/`

The Mining Company has developed more than 200 World Wide Web guides in a variety of topical areas. The Mental Health guide was developed by Leonard Holmes, a clinical psychologist in private practice who also provides mental health services over the Net. The site provides links to an impressive variety of informational resources for mental health.

National Alliance for the Mentally Ill

`http://www.nami.org/`

Grassroots, self-help organization of people with serious mental illness and their families and friends. NAMI's mission is to eradicate mental illness and to improve the quality of life for those who have mental illness.

National Center for PTSD

`http://www.dartmouth.edu/dms/ptsd/`

U.S. Department of Veterans Affairs National Center for PTSD offers research and education on Post-Traumatic Stress Disorder.

National Institute of Mental Health

`http://www.nimh.nih.gov/`

General information about NIMH, public information about mental health, including quicktime videos, news and announcements from NIMH, grants, contracts, and committee information, and information on NIMH research activities.

National Mental Health Association

`http://www.nmha.org/`

The National Mental Health Association, through its national office and more than 300 affiliates nationwide, is dedicated to improving the mental health of all individuals and achieving victory over mental illnesses.

part

2

National Panic-Anxiety Disorder News

http://www.npadnews.com/

NPAD News presents research, self-help techniques, new books and tapes, studies, conferences and more for people with Panic/Anxiety disorders.

Post Traumatic Stress Resources

http://www.long-beach.va.gov/ptsd/stress.html

The purpose of the Post Traumatic Stress Web Resources Page is to list and maintain information and links to professional information on the Post Traumatic Stress Syndrome from whatever cause. The site is created and maintained by the PTSD Program of the Department of Psychiatry, Carl T. Hayden VAMC, Phoenix Arizona.

Psychiatry On-Line

http://www.priory.co.uk/psych.htm

The International Forum for Psychiatry—a peer reviewed, independent psychiatry journal for psychiatrists and mental health professionals. Contains articles, archives, and links to professional resources.

Social Work Practice Update: Recovered Memories

http://members.aol.com/NASWKY/memories.html

NASW's National Council on the Practice of Clinical Social Work published this practice update on Evaluation and Treatment of Adults with the possibility of Recovered Memories of Childhood Sexual Abuse.

Specifica Mental Health Resources

http://www.realtime.net/~mmjw/

A topical list of references for consumers by Jeanine Wade, Ph.D.

Stress Free

http://www.stressfree.com/

StressFree Net offers stress related services and tools, including a directory of health and stress management professionals to help the user, and an opportunity to "Ask the Psychologist."

part

2

Screening for Suicide Risk

http://cpmcnet.columbia.edu/texts/gcps/gcps0060.html

Important information on screening for suicide intent from Columbia-Presbyterian Medical Center.

Therapist Referral Network

http://dbmac.dbcity.com/trn/

TRN is a free service providing users with information to help them search for licensed psychotherapists and other mental health services. The program allows a detailed search for licensed professionals by location based on specialization, fee, insurance plan, theoretical orientation, and more.

UCLA School Mental Health Project

http://smhp.psych.ucla.edu/

The School Mental Health Project (SMHP) was created to pursue theory, research, practice and training related to meeting the mental health needs of youngsters through school-based interventions. Their award winning Web site offers information on our clearinghouse, introductory packets, consultation cadre, newsletter, links to other Internet sites and electronic networking.

part
2

WEBster's Death, Dying and Grief Guide

http://www.katsden.com/death/

This Web site represents a large and comprehensive collection of Internet resources with a holistic perspective. It is focused on death as "natural" and expected for all living beings.

The Wounded Healer Journal

http://idealist.com/wounded_healer/

Issues of grief and loss for survivors of sexual abuse.

POLICY PRACTICE

Action Alert: Welfare Reform

http://www.now.org/issues/economic/welfref.html

The National Organization for Women presents a policy analysis relating welfare reform and domestic violence.

Behaviorists for Social Responsibility

http://www.bfsr.org/

BFSR is a Special Interest Group of the Association for Behavior Analysis. The SIG and the site are dedicated to applications of the science of behavior and cultural analysis to issues of social importance, including education, human rights, environmental and social justice issues. The site includes links to related state-of-the art publications and related sites.

Canadian Centre for Policy Alternatives

http://www.policyalternatives.ca/

The Canadian Centre for Policy Alternatives was founded in 1980 to promote research on economic and social issues facing Canada. The Centre monitors current developments in the economy and studies important trends that affect Canadians. The Web site provides information about the activities of the center, its publications and links to related resources.

Canadian Council on Social Development

http://www.ccsd.ca/

The Canadian Council on Social Development is a voluntary, nonprofit organization whose mission is to develop and promote progressive social policies inspired by social justice, equality and the empowerment of individuals and communities through research, consultation, public education and advocacy. The Web site features information about the center and access to its statistical databases.

Centre for Social Policy Research and Development

http://www.bangor.ac.uk/csprd/home.htm

The Centre for Social Policy Research and Development (CSPRD) at the University of Wales, Bangor, is committed to the conduct of well-founded, scientific research primarily in the areas of human development, health studies and social care provision. The site offers information about the center, research reports, and links to related resources.

Congress.org—A Guide to the U.S. Congress

http://congress.org

Congress.org is an updated online directory of information for both the US House of Representatives and the US Senate. A comprehensive resource for communicating with Congress, the structure and features of Congress.org can be customized to the needs of any organization or business involved in public affairs or grassroots activities.

Contacting the Congress

http://www.visi.com/juan/congress

Contacting the Congress is a listing of phone numbers, fax numbers, electronic mail addresses and WWW/Gopher home pages for members of the Congress.

The Electronic Activist

http://www.berkshire.net/~ifas/activist/

An email address directory of congresspeople, state governments, and media, from the Institute for First Amendment Studies.

Electronic Policy Network

http://epn.org/

EPN considers itself to be the clearinghouse for the latest progressive policy research and reports from the nation's leading research institutes, think tanks, and policy organizations. The site provides online compendia of news and individual policy issues, a search engine, access to a mailing list to keep up with policy developments as they happen, and topical links to member institutions and beyond.

part

2

Federal News Service

http://www.fnsg.com/

FNS allows you to read the actual words spoken by national leaders on matters of official U.S. Government policy and other issues of the day, the same day.

MIMH/PIE Confluence Page

http://pie.org/

A joint project of the Missouri Institute of Mental Health and the Policy Information Exchange, this is a comprehensive mental health policy Internet resource. The MIMH side of the site provides information about the activities of the center, which is housed at the University of Missouri-Columbia. It also provides links to related sites, consumer information, and access to its publications. PIE Online is one of the largest online collections of health and mental health policy information available anywhere. Textual and statistical information, documents, bibliographies, reviews, federal and state legislative information, job and funding opportunities, and events calendars can be found quickly using PIE Online's full text retrieval capabilities. PIE is available by subscription only, which may be the way of the future on the Internet.

PoliticsOnline

http://www.politicsonline.com/

This site is devoted to providing tools, tips and news about how to use the Internet to make political communications more effective.

PRAXIS

http://www.ssw.upenn.edu/~restes/praxis.html

The international development home page of Prof. Richard J. Estes of the University of Pennsylvania, this site to an array of archival resources on international and comparative social development designed to meet the informational needs of social work educators and students with international interests and other educators and students who require assistance in locating useful national and international resources on social and economic development.

Project Vote Smart

http://www.vote-smart.org

Project Vote Smart tracks the performance of over 13,000 political leaders, including the President, Congress, Governors, and State Legislatures.

United Nations Development Program

http://www.undp.org/

UNDP's overarching mission is to help countries build national capacity to achieve sustainable, human development, giving top priority to eliminating poverty and building equity.

The University of Michigan School of Public Policy

http://www.spp.umich.edu/

Formerly the Institute for Public Policy Studies, the School of Public Policy became an independent school within the University of Michigan in 1995. In addition to providing information about the programs offered by the School of Public Policy, the site also provides a working paper archive.

part 2

Welfare Policy Center

http://www.hudson.org/wpc/

The Welfare Policy Center (WPC) conducts research and provides technical assistance on welfare reform and related issues. It is a resource for policymakers, program administrators, the press, and many others seeking to learn about cutting-edge welfare reforms and what it takes to make reforms effective. This Web site provides information about key welfare issues and interesting welfare-related articles.

Welfare Reform Introduction

http://www.epn.org/tcf/welfintr.html

This site is designed to substitute facts for myth in the important public battle over welfare reform. The Twentieth Century Fund is a nonprofit, nonpartisan foundation that sponsors and supervises research on economic, social, and political issues. Contributors to the information presented on the site include Joel Handler, Professor of Law, University of California, Los Angeles; Yeheskel Hasenfeld, Professor of Social Welfare, University of California, Los Angeles; and Jack Sirica of *Newsday*.

The Welfare to Work Partnership

http://www.welfaretowork.org/

The Welfare to Work Partnership (The Partnership) was launched on May 20,1997 at the White House by President Clinton, Governors Tommy Thompson (R–WI) and Tom Carper (D–DE) and over 100 participating businesses. This national, nonpartisan, not-for-profit organization was created to encourage and assist businesses hiring individuals from public assistance without displacing current workers.

Western New York Law Center

http://www.wnylc.com/

The Western New York Law Center maintains StarWatch, a Web site designed to assist welfare advocates with helpful information.

PREVENTION

part
2

The Abuse Prevention Project

http://www.pacer.org/app/abusea.htm

This Minneapolis-based program provides resources to families and professionals for the prevention of child abuse with a focus on disability and cultural competency.

Child Abuse Prevention Network

http://child.cornell.edu/

An initiative of Family Life Development Center at Cornell University. The network is dedicated to enhancing Internet resources for the prevention of child abuse and neglect, and reducing the negative conditions in the family and the community that lead to child maltreatment.

Committee for Children

http://www.cfchildren.org/

Committee for Children provides classroom curricula for the prevention of child abuse and youth violence as well as training and parent education. They also conduct original research evaluating the effectiveness of their programs.

Community Psychology Network

http://www.cmmtypsych.net

Community Psychology Net is the Web's most comprehensive site dedicated to the field of community psychology. This site is meant to be a resource for educators, professionals, researchers, graduate and undergraduate students, and others who are interested in learning more about the fascinating field of community psychology, action research, intervention, and prevention. The site provides links to discussion lists, professional membership groups, graduate schools, course materials, funding sources, position announcements, social policy information, and various other miscellaneous resources relevant to the field.

Early Career Preventionists Network

http://tigger.oslc.org/Ecpn/

Providing information, educational experiences, and networking opportunities for researchers, interventionists, and advocates dedicated to the science of prevention.

part
2

National Clearinghouse on Child Abuse and Neglect

http://www.calib.com/nccanch/

Supported by the Children's Bureau, The National Clearinghouse on Child Abuse and Neglect Information is a national resource for professionals seeking information on the prevention, identification, and treatment of child abuse and neglect, and related child welfare issues.

National Drug Prevention League

http://www.ndpl.org/

The NDPL is an association of over 25 national and major regional private sector organizations for drug abuse prevention. The site provides links to related resources and information, including national surveys and studies, federal programs and budgets and congressional bills.

Parents Anonymous

http://www.parentsanonymous-natl.org/

Parents Anonymous is the nation's oldest and largest child abuse prevention organization dedicated to strengthening families through innovative strategies that promote mutual support and parent leadership.

Partnership for a Drug-Free America

http://www.drugfreeamerica.org/

This site includes a comprehensive database of drug information: what they do, what they look like, their history, and slang terms.

RESEARCH AND MEASUREMENT

Alcoholism Treatment Assessment Instruments

part
2

http://silk.nih.gov/silk/niaaa1/publication/assinstr.htm

Information on the availability of a variety of instruments for adolescents and adults to be used in screening, diagnosis, assessment of drinking behavior, treatment planning, treatment and process assessment, and outcome evaluation.

Allyn and Bacon's Sociology Links

http://www.fsu.edu/~crimdo/soclinks/research.html

Provides links to sites related to research methods.

AlphaLogic

http://www.travel-net.com/~alphalog/

Presents the Personality Diagnostic Questionnaire (PDQ-4), a user-friendly interactive program that determines the presence of personality disorders consistent with the DSM-IV, Axis II.

American Evaluation Association

http://www.eval.org/

An international professional association of evaluators devoted to the application and exploration of program evaluation, personnel evaluation, technology, and other forms of evaluation.

American Institutes for Research

http://www.air-dc.org/

AIR is an independent, not-for-profit corporation that performs basic and applied research, provides technical support, and conducts analyses in the behavioral and social sciences.

APA: FAQ on Psychological Tests

http://www.apa.org/science/test.html

American Psychological Association provides answers to Frequently Asked Questions about the selection and use of psychological tests.

American Sociological Association Section on Methods

http://lion.icpsr.umich.edu/methsect/

Provides information about the activities of the section.

part

2

ANU—Coombspapers FTP Archive

http://coombs.anu.edu.au/CoombswebPages/Coombspapers.html

This archive site was established to act as an electronic repository of the social science and humanities papers, bibliographies, directories, theses abstracts and other high-grade research material produced (or deposited) at the Research Schools of Social Sciences and Pacific and Asian Studies, Australian National University, Canberra, Australia.

Buros Institute of Mental Measurements

http://www.unl.edu/buros/

Comprehensive site providing reviews of tests, links to important resources for testing, and standards for utilization of tests.

Census and Demographic Data

http://www.clark.net/pub/lschank/web/census.html

A wonderful resource page for people working with census and other demographic data.

Center for Demography and Ecology

http://www.ssc.wisc.edu/cde/

CDE is a multi-disciplinary faculty research cooperative for social scientific demographic research whose membership includes sociologists, rural sociologists, economists, and historians.

Center for Social Research Methods

http://trochim.human.cornell.edu/

This Web site, developed by Bill Trochim at Cornell, is intended for people involved in applied social research and evaluation. There are many links to other locations on the Web that deal in applied social research methods, previously published and unpublished papers, detailed examples of current research projects, useful tools for researchers (like a guide to selecting a statistical analysis), an extensive online textbook, a bulletin board for discussions, and more.

Cochrane Collaboration

http://hiru.mcmaster.ca/cochrane/

Facilitates the creative, review, maintenance and dissemination of systematic overviews of the effects of health care.

Community of Science

http://www.cos.com/

The mission of the Community of Science (COS) is to provide rapid, easy-to-use information about scientists and the funding of science. The Community of Science is a global registry designed to provide accurate, timely, easy-to-access information about what new funding opportunities exist, and who is working on what subject, and where.

Content Analysis

`http://www.gsu.edu/~wwwcom/content.html`

Resources to assist researchers utilizing content analysis strategies, including reviews of publications, bilbiographies, and software.

Corporate Grantmakers on the Internet

`http://fdncenter.org/2grntmkr/2corp.html`

Annotated listing of interests and geographic limitationsof scores of company-sponsored private foundations and direct corporate giving programs.

CSAC Ethnographics Gallery Software Archives

`http://lucy.ukc.ac.uk/archives.html`

Shareware statistics program, SchoolStat™. Graphic display of probability distributions, spread sheet, and a variety of parametric and nonparametric statistics.

ERIC Clearinghouse on Assessment and Evaluation

`http://www.ericae.net/`

Information pertaining to educational and psychological testing and learning theories. Provides balanced information concerning educational assessment and resources to encourage responsible test use.

Finding Information about Psychological Tests: Frequently Asked Questions (FAQ)

`http://www.apa.org/science/test.html`

The American Psychological Association Science Directorate answers hundreds of calls and letters each year from persons trying to locate the right test or find more information about psychological tests. APA neither sells nor endorses testing instruments, but it does provide guidance in using available resources to find psychological tests. Answers to Frequently Asked Questions are provided here.

part

2

Funding Institutions—Foundations

http://resource.ca.jhu.edu/foundations.html

A listing of foundations from Johns Hopkins University.

Geriatric Assessment Methods

http://text.nlm.nih.gov/nih/cdc/www/65txt.html

Discusses various aspects of data-based decision making for care decisions with geriatric patients.

Geriatric Depression Scale

http://www.vh.org/Providers/ClinRef/FPHandbook/Chapter15/01-15.html#Box15-2

Scale measuring depression in elderly subjects.

part
2

Glossary of Computing and Social Science Terms

http://odwin.ucsd.edu/glossary/

Covers terms which may be useful in managing data collections and providing basic data services.

Human Subjects in Research Sites

http://www.psych.bangor.ac.uk/deptpsych/Ethics/HumanResearch.html

This page is intended to provide pointers to information about ethical aspects of research involving human subjects as participants.

Idea Works, Inc.

http://www.ideaworks.com/ideaworks

An information technology company specializing in the development and publication of expert systems for business, industry, research, and human services. Services include training, consulting, development, publication, and contract services.

The Illinois Researcher Information Service (IRIS)

http://www.library.uiuc.edu/iris/

The Illinois Researcher Information Service (IRIS) is a unit of the University of Illinois Library at Urbana-Champaign. The IRIS office compiles the IRIS database of funding opportunities. The office also maintains a library of publications (informational brochures, application guidelines, and annual reports) from over 2,000 funding agencies.

Institute for Social Research

http://www.isr.umich.edu/

Information about the research facility at the University of Michigan. Includes the Survey Research Center, the Research Center for Group Dynamics, and the Center for Political Studies.

Internal Validity Tutorial

http://server.bmod.athabascau.ca/html/Validity/

This self-instructional tutorial on internal validity that teaches students to recognize and analyze flaws in the design of clinical experiments.

part 2

International Index of Social Progress

http://newciv.org/GIB/BOV/BV-377.HTML

Measures economic development, social and political conditions, and the ability of nations to produce welfare services for their citizens.

Internet Resources for Institutional Research

http://apollo.gmu.edu/~jmilam/air95.html

Annotated links to assist institutional researchers and faculty and students in higher education in navigating the Internet.

Mathematical and Statistical Software

http://portal.research.bell-labs.com/cgi-wald/dbaccess/32

A searchable database of public domain software, available through the "netlib" server available through research at AT&T Bell Laboratories Murray Hill, and the University of Tennessee.

Methods Resources

http://research.ed.asu.edu/

Research methods resources from the College of Education at Arizona State University.

National Institutes of Health Funding Opportunities

http://www.nih.gov/grants/

Information about NIH grant and fellowship programs, applying for a grant or fellowship, policy changes, administrative responsibilities of awardees, the CRISP database, and the numbers and characteristics of awards made by the NIH.

On Being a Scientist: Responsible Conduct in Research

http://www.nap.edu/readingroom/books/obas/

An online publication of the Committee on Science, Engineering, and Public Policy of the National Academy of Sciences.

part
2

OpinionMeter

http://www.opinionmeter.com/

Interactive fully-automated polling machine to measure customer satisfaction.

Power Analysis

http://hedwig.mgh.harvard.edu/size.html

Statistical considerations for determining sample size, power, and the minimal detectable difference in clinical trials and scientific experiments.

Power Calculator

http://www.stat.ucla.edu/~jbond/HTMLPOWER/

Web-based software to determine statistical power.

Private Foundations on the Internet

http://fdncenter.org/2grntmkr/2priv.html

Annotated listing detailing interests and geographical limitations of hundreds of private foundations.

ProGAMMA: Social Science Information Technology

http://www.gamma.rug.nl/

Information Technology for the Social and Behavioral sciences (SSIT)

Psychological Maltreatment of Women Inventory

http://www.umich.edu/~rtolman/pmwimas.htm

Created by Richard Tolman at University of Michigan to investigate woman abuse.

Qualitative Methods (QualPage)

part
2

http://www.ualberta.ca/~jrnorris/qual.html

Resources for qualitative researchers.

RAMS-FIE

http://web.fie.com/

RAMS-FIE is the result of an October 1st, 1996, merger between Research Administration Management Systems, Inc. and Federal Information Exchange, Inc. Together they form a diversified information services company providing a full range of database services, software development and technical support to the government, private sector and academic communities.

RAND

http://www.rand.org/

Through research and analysis, RAND assists public policymakers at all levels, private sector leaders in many industries, and the public at large in efforts to strengthen the nation's economy, maintain its security, and improve its quality of life.

RAND-36 Health Survey Trial

http://www.mcw.edu/midas/health/

A new short-form health survey, which taps eight health concepts: physical functioning, bodily pain, role limitations due to physical health problems, role limitations due to personal or emotional problems, general mental health, social functioning, energy/fatigue, and general health perceptions.

Russell Sage Foundation

http://epn.org/sage/

The principal American foundation devoted exclusively to research in the social sciences, the Foundation is a research center, a funding source for studies by scholars at other academic and research institutions, and an active member of the nation's social science community.

part
2

Social Science Research Center

http://www.ssrc.msstate.edu/Publications/

The SSRC at Mississippi State University makes available many of their research reports on this site.

Society for Judgment and Decision-Making

http://www.sjdm.org/

The Society for Judgment and Decision Making is an interdisciplinary organization dedicated to the study of normative, descriptive, and prescriptive theories of decision.

StatLib

http://www.stat.cmu.edu/

StatLib is a system for distributing statistical software, datasets, and information by email, FTP, and WWW. It is a service of the Carnegie Mellon University Statistics Department.

Statistical Power Analysis Software

http://sustain.forestry.ubc.ca/cacb/power/index.html

Provides an up-to-date list of microcomputer software that can be used to calculate the power of statistical hypothesis tests.

Statistical Resources on the Internet

`http://www.cas.vt.edu/Statistics/resource.html`

It is provided as a starting point for locating statistical related information on the World Wide Web.

Statistical Software Support

`http://www.aom.pace.edu/rmd/statsoft.html`

Part of the Research Methods Web site at the Academy of Management.

The Statistics Home Page

`http://www.statsoftinc.com/textbook/stathome.html`

This Electronic Statistical Textbook offers training in the understanding and application of statistics. The material was developed at the StatSoft RandD department based on many years of teaching undergraduate and graduate statistics courses and covers a wide variety of applications, including laboratory research, business statistics and forecasting, social science statistics and survey research, data mining, engineering and quality control applications.

part
2

Substance Abuse Subtle Screening Inventory

`http://www.cerainc.com/html/sas.html`

Substance abuse screening from Consultation, Education, and Research Associates.

University Center for Urban and Social Research

`http://info.pitt.edu/~ucsur/`

Established at University of Pittsburgh to carry out basic and applied social science research, the UCSUR is a focal point for collaborative interdisciplinary and multidisciplinary approaches to social science and policy issues.

Web Resources for Educational Research and Evaluation

`http://www-leland.stanford.edu/~davidf/webresources.html`

An excellent set of links, most of which are equally applicable to social work research and evaluation, maintained by David Fetterman

The World-Wide Web Virtual Library: Statistics

http://www.stat.ufl.edu/vlib/statistics.html

A cornucopia of links related to statistics.

SEXUALITY

Able-Together

http://www.well.com/user/blaine/abletog.html

ABLE-TOGETHER is a quarterly international newsletter for bisexual and gay men with and without disabilities. The site offers links to Web sites on disability and sexuality.

Coalition for Positive Sexuality

http://www.positive.org/cps/

The Coalition for Positive Sexuality was formed to give teens the information about sexuality they need to take care of themselves and affirm their decisions about sex, sexuality, and reproductive control. They also hope to facilitate dialogue, in and out of the public schools, on condom availability and sex education. Just Say Yes, their irreverent and unabashed comprehensive sex education guide is available here.

Collected Domestic Partner Information

http://www.cs.cmu.edu/afs/cs.cmu.edu/user/scotts/
domestic-partners

A collection of information about the issues of domestic partner policies, same sex marriages, and adoption.

The Data Lounge: Lesbian/Gay Internet

http://www.datalounge.com/

Daily News, Culture and Gossip, Forums and Weekly Surveys. Global Lesbian/Gay Calendar. Web Directory and Edwina's Dating Service.

Deaf Queer Resource Center

http://www.deafqueer.org/

DQRC is a national nonprofit information center. Considered to be "the place" to find comprehensive and accurate information about the deaf queer community.

Gay, Bisexual, Lesbian and Transgender Information

http://www.abdn.ac.uk/~csc145/Gay-rights.html

Offers links to GBLT resources internationally.

Gay Canada

http://www.cglbrd.com/

The first and only GLB community based information network for Canadian gays, lesbians, and bisexuals, this site contains a wealth of resources, updated frequently.

The Gay Connection

http://www.thegayconnection.com/

A gay, lesbian, bisexual one-stop resource site.

part

2

Gay, Lesbian and Bisexual Issues Links

http://wanda.pond.com/~stevecap/glb.htm

An extensive listing of resources for gay men and lesbians, bisexual men and women, and transgendered individuals.

!OutProud!

http://www.outproud.org/

This the WWW site for the National Coalition for Gay, Lesbian, and Bisexual Youth. The site offers a wide range of resources for youth and educators.

Queer Frontiers

http://www.usc.edu/isd/archives/queerfrontiers/
queer/beyond/

1995 Conference Proceedings and Beyond: A Scholarly Resource for Queer Theory and Studies. The focus of ongoing content development for "Beyond 1995" is on a queer theoretically focused investigation, analysis and critique of the Internet's cultural and social significance and impact and how it is itself generating a whole new cyber-culture and subsequent cyber-reality.

Transgender Forum

http://www.tgfmall.com/

A resource guide for crossdressers, transvestites, transsexuals, transgendered people, their family and friends.

Youth Assistance Organization/Youth Action Online

http://youth.org/

This is a service run by volunteers, created to help self-identifying gay, lesbian, bisexual and questioning youth. YAO exists to provide young people with a safe space online to be themselves. The site offers information for youths questioning their sexuality, an online magazine, and links to other resources on the Internet.

SUBSTANCE ABUSE

Addiction Research Foundation

http://www.arf.org/

The ARF, founded in 1949, is one of North America's pre-eminent facilities for research into alcohol, tobacco and other drug problems. The Foundation's mission is to work with its partners to create and apply knowledge to prevent and reduce substance abuse in Ontario. The ARF collaborates with the World Health Organization, participating in international research and carrying out training programs in other countries.

Alcoholics Anonymous

http://www.alcoholics-anonymous.org/

Information about the self-help organization.

AL-ANON and ALATEEN

http://www.Al-Anon-Alateen.org/

These are worldwide organizations that offer self-help recovery programs for families and friends of alcoholics whether or not the alcoholic seeks help or even recognizes the existence of a drinking problem.

American Society of Addiction Medicine

http://207.201.181.5/

The medical specialty society dedicated to educating physicians and improving the treatment of individuals suffering from alcoholism or other addictions.

AMERSA

http://center.butler.brown.edu/AMERSA/

Association for Medical Education and Research in Substance Abuse, sponsored by the Center for Alcohol and Addiction Studies at Brown University.

part

2

APA Division 28

http://www.apa.org/divisions/div28/

American Psychological Association Division 28 is the special interest group for psychopharmacology and Substance Abuse. This page offers their archives and information on research opportunities.

Canadian Centre on Substance Abuse

http://www.ccsa.ca/

A nonprofit organization working to minimize the harm associated with the use of alcohol, tobacco and other drugs, this site offers links to a wealth of resources, including online courses on substance abuse topics.

Center for Alcohol and Addiction Studies

http://center.butler.brown.edu/

Features information about the work of the center and links to related resources.

Center for Education and Drug Abuse Research

http://info.pitt.edu/~mmv/cedar.html

Information on CEDAR, an ongoing 20-year prospective family/high-risk study of substance abuse, including grant information, description of the design and research modules, list of publications, news, and links to other drug-related resources.

Center for Substance Abuse Prevention

http://www.covesoft.com/csap.html

CSAP Technical Assistance Services to Communities is a unique federally funded program designed to disseminate information, increase dialog, and promote community empowerment to combat alcohol and other drug problems.

Cocaine Anonymous

http://www.ca.org/

Cocaine Anonymous is a 12-step fellowship of men and women who share their experience, strength and hope with each other so that they may solve their common problem and help others to recover from their addiction.

Dual Diagnosis Web Site

http://www.erols.com/ksciacca/

Dual Diagnosis refers to co-occurring Mental Illness, Drug Addiction and/or Alcoholism in various combinations. This site is designed to provide information and resources for service providers, consumers, and family members who are seeking assistance and/or education in this field.

Narcotics Anonymous

http://na.org/

Narcotics Anonymous is an international, community-based association of recovering drug addicts. Started in 1947, the NA movement is one of the world's oldest and largest of its type, with nearly twenty thousand weekly meetings in seventy countries.

part

2

National Alliance of Methadone Advocates

http://www.methadone.org/

NAMA is an organization composed of methadone maintenance patients and supporters of quality methadone maintenance treatment.

National Association of Alcoholism and Drug Abuse Counselors

http://www.naadac.org/

NAADAC'S mission is to provide leadership in the alcoholism and drug abuse counseling profession. The site offers information about the organization and links to important resources.

National Clearinghouse for Alcohol and Drug Information

http://www.health.org/

Offers electronic access to searchable databases and substance abuse prevention materials that pertain to alcohol, tobacco, and drugs.

**part
2**

National Organization on Fetal Alcohol Syndrome

http://www.nofas.org/

NOFAS is a nonprofit organization dedicated to eliminating birth defects caused by alcohol consumption during pregnancy and improving the quality of life for those individuals and families affected. NOFAS is the only national organization focusing solely on FAS, the leading known cause of mental retardation.

Nicotine and Tobacco Network

http://tobacco.arizona.edu/

NicNet is sponsored by the Arizona Program for Nicotine and Tobacco Research at the University of Arizona. This page is a great place to visit to find resources on quitting and for general information about quitting smoking.

The Research Institute on Addictions

http://www.ria.org/

RIA in Buffalo, New York, is a national leader in alcohol and substance abuse prevention, treatment, and policy research. The site offers information about the work of the center, including its Minority Research Development Program.

Secular Organizations for Sobriety

http://www.unhooked.com/

SOS is an alternative recovery method for those alcoholics or drug addicts who are uncomfortable with the spiritual content of widely available 12-Step programs.

Sobriety and Recovery Resources

http://www.winternet.com/~terrym/sobriety.html

Links to personal testimonials and information about self-help, largely 12-step, groups.

Substance Abuse and Mental Health Services Administration

http://www.samhsa.gov/

The SAMHSA home page offers links to a wide variety of resources.

Web of Addictions

http://www.well.com/user/woa/

The Web of Addictions is dedicated to providing accurate information about alcohol and other drug addictions and a resource for teachers, students and others who need factual information about abused drugs.

VIOLENCE

Act Against Violence Outreach Campaign

http://www.krma.org/aav/

Act Against Violence is a two-year, statewide campaign to educate the public about violence and to provide individuals and community organizations with information that encourages collaborative, community-based prevention activities.

Assault Prevention Information Network

`http://ccwf.cc.utexas.edu/~weiss/`

Information about the work of the Network, self-defense resources, martial arts resources, information about violence in society and violence prevention.

Bureau of Justice Statistics Crime and Victims Statistics

`http://www.ojp.usdoj.gov/bjs/cvict.htm`

Information, statistics, and publications about criminal victimization in the United States and related data collections.

Child Abuse Prevention Network

`http://child.cornell.edu/`

This site is dedicated to using the World Wide Web to give child abuse prevention professionals the fullest possible support in their work A seemingly inexhaustible reference of links for professionals.

Comunity United Against Violence

`http://www.xq.com/cuav/`

CUAV is a 15 year old nonprofit agency which addresses and prevents hate violence directed at lesbians, gay men, bisexuals, and transgender persons.

Domestic Violence Handbook

`http://www.domesticviolence.org/`

This online resource is designed to assist women who are experiencing domestic abuse.

Domestic Violence Hotlines

`http://www.feminist.org/911/crisis.html`

Links to telephone, postal, and electronic addresses for domestic violence hotlines across the country.

part

2

The Family Peace Project

http://www.family.mcw.edu/ahec/ec/dom_vi_h.html

The Family Peace Project provides education, training and consultation to citizens, health care professionals, organizations and communities. Staff for the Project consists of psychologists and community activists who believe that citizens can improve their communities by using the power of individual responsibility, civic action and the democratic process to engage the strengths and resources of our local communities and create local solutions.

Family Violence Prevention Fund

http://www.fvpf.org/fund/

FUND is a national nonprofit organization that focuses on domestic violence education, prevention and public policy reform.

Guggenheim Foundation Research on Violence and Aggression

http://www.hfg.org/

The Harry Frank Guggenheim Foundation sponsors scholarly research on problems of violence, aggression, and dominance. The foundation provides both research grants to established scholars and dissertation fellowships to graduate students during the dissertation-writing year. The *HFG Review* of research is published on a semi-annual basis.

GUNFREE

http://www.gunfree.org/

The Coalition to Stop Gun Violence was founded to combat the growing gun violence problem in the United States. CSGV is a unique coalition of more than forty religious, professional, labor, medical, educational and civic organizations.

Justice Information Center (NCJRS): Victims Domestic and Family Violence

http://www.ncjrs.org/victdv.htm

Links to documents about domestic and family violence.

Minnesota Higher Education Center Against Violence and Abuse

http://www.mincava.umn.edu/

The goal of the Clearinghouse is to provide a quick and user friendly access point to the extensive electronic resources on the topic of violence and abuse available through the Internet. It offers access to thousands of Gopher servers, interactive discussion groups, newsgroups and Web sites around the world.

National Campaign to Reduce Youth Violence

http://www.wnet.org/aav/index.html

Initiated by public broadcasting, this is a multiyear effort to reduce youth violence in our communities. In addition to presenting programming, the campaign is working with community-based and national organizations on community development and outreach activities.

National Coalition Against Domestic Violence

http://www.webmerchants.com/ncadv/

NCADV is a grassroots nonprofit membership organization working since 1978 to end violence in the lives of women and children. They provide a national network for state coalitions and local programs serving battered women and their children, public policy at the national level, technical assistance, community awareness campaigns, general information and referrals, and publications on the issue of domestic violence, sponsor of a national conference every two years for battered women and their advocates.

National Consortium on Violence Research

http://www.ncovr.heinz.cmu.edu/

NCOVR has been created as a research and training center devoted to studying the factors contributing to inter-personal violence. The NCOVR World Wide Web site is served by the H. John Heinz III School of Public Policy and Management at Carnegie Mellon University in Pittsburgh, Pennsylvania.

part

2

National Network of Violence Prevention Practitioners

http://www.edc.org/HHD/NNVPP/

The NNVPP specializes in the preparation and distribution of curricula that synthesize violence prevention information, as well as providing specialized training and technical assistance to practitioners nationwide.

The National Victim Center

http://www.nvc.org/

The National Victim Center provides assistance to victims of crime and providers of assistance to victims of crime.

NOW and Violence Against Women

http://now.org/issues/violence

Information from the National Organization for Women about violence against women.

Pacific Center for Violence Prevention

http://www.pcvp.org/

The Pacific Center for Violence Prevention, a project of the Trauma Foundation, works to prevent youth violence in California. Located at San Francisco General Hospital, the Center serves as the policy head-quarters for the Violence Prevention Initiative funded by The California Wellness Foundation.

Partnerships Against Violence Network

http://pavnet.org/

PAVNET Online is a "virtual library" of information about violence and youth-at-risk, representing data from seven different federal agencies. It considers itself a "one-stop", searchable, information resource to help reduce redundancy in information management and provide clear and comprehensive access to information for states and local communities.

Rape, Abuse, and Incest National Network

http://www.rainn.org/

RAINN is a nonprofit organization based in Washington, D.C. that operates a national toll-free hotline for victims of sexual assault.

SafetyNet Domestic Violence Resources

http://www.cybergrrl.com/dv.html

A compendium of a wide range of information related to the issue of domestic violence.

Sexual Assault Information Page

http://www.cs.utk.edu/~bartley/saInfoPage.html

SAIP is a not-for-profit information and referral which provides information concerning acquaintance rape, child sexual abuse/assault, incest, rape, ritual abuse, sexual assault, and sexual harassment. Information is provided via the WWW, email, a bi-monthly electronic newsletter, as well as occasional hardcopy mailings for specific requests.

part

2

Sexual Harassment and Violence Against Women

http://www.feminist.com/sexual.htm

Links to resources about sexual harassment and violence against women.

The Silent Witness National Initiative

http://www.cybergrrl.com/dv/orgs/sw.html

In 1990, an ad hoc group of women artists and writers, upset about the growing number of women in Minnesota being murdered by their partners or acquaintances, joined together with several other women's organizations to form Arts Action Against Domestic Violence, which has as its goal the promotion of successful community-based domestic violence reduction efforts in order to reach zero domestic murders by 2010.

Stopping the Violence Against Women Bibliography

`http://www.weq.gov.bc.ca/stv/BibliographySTV.html`

A list of bibliographic references for the British Columbia Public Libraries prepared by Battered Women's Support Services, Vancouver.

Violence and Abuse in Couples Project

`http://www.ackerman.org/violence.htm`

This project has as its goal the development of a feminist-informed, morally explicit systemic conjoint treatment model to end violence by men toward their female partners.

Mailing Lists for Social Workers

Child Abuse Prevention Network

`http://child.cornell.edu/capn.html#listserv`

Mailing lists for professionals in child abuse prevention and treatment.

CJD Voice

`http://members.aol.com/larmstr853/cjdvoice/weare.htm`

Issues related to Creutzfeldt-Jakob Disease.

cti-soc-work-uk

`http://www.mailbase.ac.uk/lists-a-e/cti-soc-work-uk/`

CTI Human Services maintain this list to allow social work teachers in the UK, and international colleagues, to discuss the use of educational and learning technology in social work education. Information on new developments, publications, software, workshops, and conferences may also be posted.

Gender-Related Electronic Forums

`http://www-unix.umbc.edu/~korenman/wmst/forums.html`

Gender-Related Electronic Forums is an annotated, frequently-updated, award-winning listing of publicly-accessible electronic forums related to women or to gender issues.

Internet Discussion Lists for Social Workers

`http://www.rit.edu/~694www/lists.htm`

Dozens of email lists from the BPD site at Rochester Institute of Technology.

Internet Mental Health Resources

`http://freenet.msp.mn.us/ip/stockley/mental_health.html#lists`

Mailing lists for social workers in mental health.

Mental Health Net

`http://www.cmhc.com/mlists/mlists.htm`

An index of mailing lists hosted by Mental Health Net.

Mental Health Mailing Lists

`http://mentalhealth.miningco.com/library/weekly/aa060297.htm`

Mailing lists from the Mining Company.

part
2

Psychology and Support Mailing List Pointer

`http://www.grohol.com/mail.htm`

Alphabetic listing of dozens of support-oriented and professional mailings lists.

Social Work Access Network

`http://www.sc.edu/swan/listserv.html`

Nearly 50 mailing lists related to a variety of aspects of social work practice.

The Social Work Café

`http://www.geocities.com/Heartland/4862/swcafe.html`

A list of social work-related electronic mailing lists from the Social Work Café.

Social Work Listservs—Social Work Access Network (SWAN)

http://www.sc.edu/swan/listserv.html

One of the most comprehensive listings of social work relevant discussion groups is the Social Work Listservs page maintained by the SWAN.

Social Work Oncology Network

http://www.biostat.wisc.edu/aosw/swon/SWON4web.html

Issues related to oncology social work, cancer survivorship, resources for cancer survivors, psychosocial research in oncology, and issues related to AOSW.

Web Resources for Social Workers

http://www.colostate.edu/Depts/SocWork/lists.html

An extensive list of listservs from the site at Colorado State.

part

2 Documentation

 ## Your Citation for Exemplary Research

There's another detail left for us to handle—the formal citing of electronic sources in academic papers. The very factor that makes research on the Internet exciting is the same factor that makes referencing these sources challenging: their dynamic nature. A journal article exists, either in print or on microfilm, virtually forever. A document on the Internet can come, go, and change without warning. Because the purpose of citing sources is to allow another scholar to retrace your argument, a good citation allows a reader to obtain information from your primary sources, to the extent possible. This means you need to include not only information on when a source was posted on the Internet (if available) but also when you obtained the information.

The two arbiters of form for academic and scholarly writing are the Modern Language Association (MLA) and the American Psychological

Association (APA); both organizations have established styles for citing electronic publications.

MLA Style

In the fifth edition of the *MLA Handbook for Writers of Research Papers,* the MLA recommends the following formats:

- **URLs:** URLs are enclosed in angle brackets (<>) and contain the access mode identifier, the formal name for such indicators as "http" or "ftp." If a URL must be split across two lines, break it only after a slash (/). Never introduce a hyphen at the end of the first line. The URL should include all the parts necessary to identify uniquely the file/document being cited.

    `<http://www.csun.edu/~rtvfdept/home/index.html>`

- **An online scholarly project or reference database:** A complete online reference contains the title of the project or database (underlined); the name of the editor of the project or database (if given); electronic publication information, including version number (if relevant and if not part of the title), date of electronic publication or latest update, and name of any sponsoring institution or organization; date of access; and electronic address.

`The Perseus Project`. Ed. Gregory R. Crane.
    Mar. 1997. Department of Classics, Tufts University. 15 June 1998 <http://www.perseus.tufts.edu/>.

If you cannot find some of the information, then include the information that is available. The MLA also recommends that you print or download electronic documents, freezing them in time for future reference.

- **A document within a scholarly project or reference database:** It is much more common to use only a portion of a scholarly project or database. To cite an essay, poem, or other short work, begin this citation with the name of the author and the title of the work (in quotation marks). Then, include all the information used when citing a complete online scholarly project or reference database, however, make sure you use the URL of the specific work and not the address of the general site.

part

2

Cuthberg, Lori. "Moonwalk: Earthlings' Finest Hour."
    Discovery Channel Online. 1999. Discovery
    Channel. 25 Nov. 1999 <http://www.discovery.com/
    indep/newsfeatures/moonwa lk/challenge.html>.

■ **A professional or personal site:** Include the name of the person creating the site (reversed), followed by a period, the title of the site
(underlined), or, if there is no title, a description such as Home page
(such a description is neither placed in quotes nor underlined). Then,
specify the name of any school, organization, or other institution affiliated with the site and follow it with your date of access and the
URL of the page.

O'Connor, Tom. Megalinks in Criminal Justice. North
    Carolina Wesleyan College. 4 Jan. 2000
    <http://faculty.ncwc.edu/toconnor/>.

Some electronic references are truly unique to the online domain.
These include email, newsgroup postings, MUDs (multiuser domains)
or MOOs (multiuser domains, object-oriented), and IRCs (Internet
Relay Chats).

Email   In citing email messages, begin with the writer's name (reversed) followed by a period, then the title of the message (if any) in
quotations as it appears in the subject line. Next comes a description of
the message, typically "Email to," and the recipient (e.g., "the author"),
and finally the date of the message.

Davis, Jeffrey. "Web Writing Resources." Email to
    Nora Davis. 3 Jan. 2000.

Sommers, Laurice. "Re: College Admissions Practices."
    Email to the author. 12 Dec. 1999.

List Servers and Newsgroups   In citing these references, begin with the
author's name (reversed) followed by a period. Next include the title of
the document (in quotes) from the subject line, followed by the words
"Online posting" (not in quotes). Follow this with the date of posting.
For list servers, include the date of access, the name of the list (if
known), and the online address of the list's moderator or administrator.
For newsgroups, follow "Online posting" with the date of posting, the

date of access, and the name of the newsgroup, prefixed with news: and enclosed in angle brackets.

```
Applebaum, Dale. "Educational Variables." Online
    posting. 29 Jan. 1998. Higher Education
    Discussion Group. 30 January 1993
    <jlucidoj@unc.edu>.

Gostl, Jack. "Re: Mr. Levitan." Online posting.
    13 June 1997. 20 June 1997
    <news:alt.edu.bronxscience>.
```

MUDs, MOOs, and IRCs   Citations for these online sources take the form of the name of the speaker(s) followed by a period. Then comes the description and date of the event, the forum in which the communication took place, the date of access, and the online address prefixed by "telnet//".

```
Guest. Personal interview. 24 December 1999.
    LinguaMOO. 24 December 1999 <telnet://du.edu:8888>.
```

part 2

For more information on MLA documentation style, check out their Web site at http://www.mla.org/set_stl.htm

APA Style

The *Publication Manual of the American Psychological Association* (4th ed.) is fairly dated in its handling of online sources, having been published before the rise of the WWW and the generally recognized format for URLs. The format that follows is based on the APA manual, with modifications proposed by Russ Dewey <www.psychwww.com/resource/apacrib.htm>. It's important to remember that, unlike the MLA, the APA does not include temporary or transient sources (e.g., letters, phone calls, etc.) in its "References" page, preferring to handle them in in-text citations exclusively. This rule holds for electronic sources as well: email, MOOs/MUDs, list server postings, etc., are not included in the "References" page, merely cited in text, for example, "But Wilson has rescinded his earlier support for these policies" (Charles Wilson, personal email to the author, 20 November 1996). But also note that many list server and Usenet groups and MOOs actually archive their correspondences, so that there is a permanent site (usually a Gopher or FTP server) where those documents reside. In that case, you would want to find the archive and cite it as an unchanging source. Strictly speaking, according to the APA manual, a file from an FTP site should be referenced as follows:

```
Deutsch, P. (1991). "Archie-An electronic directory
    service for the Internet" [Online]. Available
    FTP: ftp.sura.net Directory: pub/archie/docs
    File: whatis.archie.
```

However, the increasing familiarity of Net users with the convention of a URL makes the prose description of how to find a file <"Available FTP: ftp.sura.net Directory: pub/archie/docs File: whatis.archie"> unnecessary. Simply specifying the URL should be enough.

So, with such a modification of the APA format, citations from the standard Internet sources would appear as follows.

part 2

FTP (File Transfer Protocol) Sites To cite files available for downloading via FTP, give the author's name (if known), the publication date (if available and if different from the date accessed), the full title of the paper (capitalizing only the first word and proper nouns), the address of the FTP site along with the full path necessary to access the file, and the date of access.

```
Deutsch, P. (1991) "Archie-An electronic directory
    service for the Internet." [Online]. Available:
    ftp://ftp.sura.net/pub/archie/docs/whatis.archie.
```

WWW Sites (World Wide Web) To cite files available for viewing or downloading via the World Wide Web, give the author's name (if known), the year of publication (if known and if different from the date accessed), the full title of the article, and the title of the complete work (if applicable) in italics. Include any additional information (such as versions, editions, or revisions) in parentheses immediately following the title. Include the full URL (the http address) and the date of visit.

```
Burka, L. P. (1993). A hypertext history of multi-
    user dungeons. MUDdex. http://www.utopia.com/
    talent/lpb/muddex/essay/ (13 Jan. 1997).

Tilton, J. (1995). Composing good HTML (Vers. 2.0.6).
    http://www.cs.cmu.edu/~tilt/cgh/ (1 Dec. 1996).
```

Telnet Sites List the author's name or alias (if known), the date of publication (if available and if different from the date accessed), the title of the article, the title of the full work (if applicable) or the name of the Telnet site in italics, and the complete Telnet address, followed by a comma and directions to access the publication (if applicable). Last, give the date of visit in parentheses.

```
Dava (#472). (1995, 3 November). A deadline.
   *General (#554). Internet Public Library.
   telnet://ipl.sils.umich.edu:8888, @peek 25 on
   #554 (9 Aug. 1996).

Help. Internet public library.
   telnet://ipl.org:8888/, help (1 Dec. 1996).
```

Synchronous Communications (MOOs, MUDs, IRC, etc.) Give the name of the speaker(s), the complete date of the conversation being referenced in parentheses (if different from the date accessed), and the title of the session (if applicable). Next, list the title of the site in italics, the protocol and address (if applicable), and any directions necessary to access the work. If there is additional information such as archive addresses or file numbers (if applicable), list the word "Available," a colon, and the archival information. Last, list the date of access, enclosed in parentheses. Personal interviews do not need to be listed in the References, but do need to be included in parenthetic references in the text (see the APA *Publication Manual*).

part

2

```
Basic IRC commands. irc undernet.org, /help (13 Jan.
   1996).

Cross, J. (1996, February 27). Netoric's Tuesday
   cafe: Why use MUDs in the writing classroom?
   MediaMoo. telenet://purple-crayon.media.mit.edu:
   8888, @go Tuesday. Available: ftp://daedalus.com/
   pub/ACW/NETORIC/catalog.96a (tc 022796.log).
   (1 Mar. 1996).
```

Gopher Sites List the author's name (if applicable), the year of publication (if known and if different from the date accessed), the title of the file or paper, and the title of the complete work (if applicable). Include any print publication information (if available) followed by the protocol (i.e., gopher://) and the path necessary to access the file. List the date that the file was accessed in parentheses immediately following the path.

```
Massachusetts Higher Education Coordinating
    Council. (1994) [Online]. Using coordination
    and collaboration to address change. Available:
    gopher://gopher.mass.edu:170/00gopher_root%3A%5B_
    hecc%5D_plan.
```

Email, Listservs, and Newsgroups Give the author's name (if known), the date of the correspondence in parentheses (if known and if different from the date accessed), the subject line from the posting, and the name of the list (if known) in italics. Next, list the address of the listserv or newsgroup. Include any archival information after the address, listing the word "Available" and a colon and the protocol and address of the archive. Last, give the date accessed enclosed in parentheses. Do not include personal email in the list of References. See the APA *Publication Manual* for information on in-text citations.

```
Bruckman, A. S. MOOSE crossing proposal.
    mediamoo@media.mit.edu (20 Dec. 1994).
```

```
Heilke, J. (1996, May 3). Re: Webfolios. acw-l@ttacs.
ttu.edu. Available: http://www.ttu.edu/lists/acw-l/
    9605 (31 Dec. 1996).
```

```
Laws, R. UMI thesis publication. alt.education.
    distance (3 Jan. 1996).
```

Other authors and educators have proposed similar extensions to the APA style, too. You can find URLs to these pages at

```
www.psychwww.com/resource/apacrib.htm
```

and

```
www.nouveaux.com/guides.htm
```

Another frequently-referenced set of extensions is available at

```
www.uvm.edu/~ncrane/estyles/apa.htm
```

Remember, "frequently-referenced" does not equate to "correct" or even "desirable." Check with your professor to see if your course or school has a preference for an extended APA style.

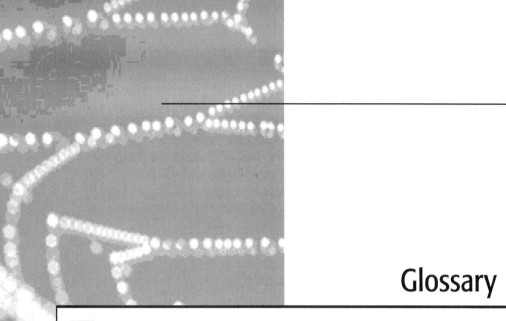

Glossary

Your Own Private Glossary

The Glossary in this book contains reference terms you'll find useful as you get started on the Internet. After a while, however, you'll find yourself running across abbreviations, acronyms, and buzzwords whose definitions will make more sense to you once you're no longer a novice (or "newbie"). That's the time to build a glossary of your own. For now, the 2DNet Webopædia gives you a place to start.

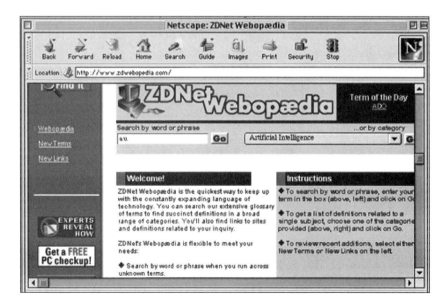

alias
A simple email address that can be used in place of a more complex one.

AVI
Audio Video Interleave. A video compression standard developed for use with Microsoft Windows. Video clips on the World Wide Web are usually available in both AVI and QuickTime formats.

bandwidth
Internet parlance for capacity to carry or transfer information such as email and Web pages.

BBS
Bulletin Board System. A dial-up computer service that allows users to post messages and download files. Some BBSs are connected to and provide access to the Internet, but many are self-contained.

browser
The computer program that lets you view the contents of Web sites.

client
A program that runs on your personal computer and supplies you with Internet services, such as getting your mail.

cyberspace
The whole universe of information that is available from computer networks. The term was coined by science fiction writer William Gibson in his novel *Neuromancer,* published in 1984.

DNS
See **domain name server.**

domain
A group of computers administered as a single unit, typically belonging to a single organization such as a university or corporation.

domain name
A name that identifies one or more computers belonging to a single domain. For example, "apple.com".

domain name server
A computer that converts domain names into the numeric addresses used on the Internet.

download
Copying a file from another computer to your computer over the Internet.

email
Electronic mail.

emoticon
A guide to the writer's feelings, represented by typed characters, such as the Smiley :-). Helps readers understand the emotions underlying a written message.

FAQ
Frequently Asked Questions

flame
A rude or derogatory message directed as a personal attack against an individual or group.

flame war
An exchange of flames (see above).

FTP
File Transfer Protocol, a method of moving files from one computer to another over the Internet.

home page
A page on the World Wide Web that acts as a starting point for information about a person or organization.

hypertext
Text that contains embedded *links* to other pages of text. Hypertext enables the reader to navigate between pages of related information by following links in the text.

LAN:
Local Area Network. A computer network that is located in a concentrated area, such as offices within a building.

link
A reference to a location on the Web that is embedded in the text of the Web page. Links are usually highlighted with a different color or underline to make them easily visible.

list server

Strictly speaking, a computer program that administers electronic mailing lists, but also used to denote such lists or discussion groups, as in "the writer's list server."

lurker

A passive reader of an Internet *newsgroup*. A lurker reads messages, but does not participate in the discussion by posting or responding to messages.

mailing list

A subject-specific automated e-mail system. Users subscribe and receive e-mail from other users about the subject of the list.

modem

A device for connecting two computers over a telephone line.

newbie

A new user of the Internet.

newsgroup

A discussion forum in which all participants can read all messages and public replies between the participants.

pages

All the text, graphics, pictures, and so forth, denoted by a single URL beginning with the identifier "http://".

plug-in

A third-party software program that will lend a web browser (Netscape, Internet Explorer, etc.) additional features.

quoted

Text in an email message or newsgroup posting that has been set off by the use of vertical bars or > characters in the left-hand margin.

search engine

A computer program that will locate Web sites or files based on specified criteria.

secure
A Web page whose contents are encrypted when sending or receiving information.

server
A computer program that moves information on request, such as a Web server that sends pages to your browser.

Smiley
See **emoticon.**

snail mail
Mail sent the old fashioned way: Write a letter, put it in an envelope, stick on a stamp, and drop it in the mailbox.

spam
Spam is to the Internet as unsolicited junk mail is to the postal system.

URL
Uniform Resource Locator: The notation for specifying addresses on the World Wide Web (e.g. http://www.abacon.com or ftp://ftp.abacon.com).

Usenet
The section of the Internet devoted to *newsgroups.*

Web browser
A program used to navigate and access information on the World Wide Web. Web browsers convert html coding into a display of pictures, sound, and words.

Web site
A collection of World Wide Web pages, usually consisting of a home page and several other linked pages.